Befriending Adversity

How I Leveraged the Power of Adversity in My Life and Business

Bisi Osundeko

Contents

Dedication
Foreword
Introduction
Chapter One: Adversity Is Part of Life
- ✓ Building A Mindset and Character Development
- ✓ How Adversity Changed My Life
- ✓ Focusing on Time and Impact
- ✓ Nuggets

Chapter Two: Attitude Is Everything
- ✓ Maintaining a Positive Attitude
- ✓ Never give up
- ✓ Failure is A Teacher
- ✓ Nuggets

Chapter Three: Knowing Your Why
- ✓ Why Do You Do What You Do?

- ✓ Remember Your Original Motive
- ✓ Write the Vision and Make It Plain
- ✓ Nuggets

Chapter Four: Your Association Matters
- ✓ Surrounding Yourself with The Right People
- ✓ Who is in Your Boat?
- ✓ Nuggets

Chapter Five: You Are Not an Island
- ✓ Don't Try to Do Everything on Your Own
- ✓ Build a Passionate Team
- ✓ Before You Hire
- ✓ Nuggets

Chapter Six: First Things First
- ✓ Health, Happiness, and Well-Being

- ✓ You Need To Be Hale And Hearty
- ✓ Striking a Balance is Key
- ✓ Nuggets

Chapter Seven: You Are Not A Victim
- ✓ Get Rid of The Victim's Mentality
- ✓ Redefining your mindset
- ✓ Beyond Affliction and Adversity
- ✓ Nuggets

Chapter Eight: Immune to Adversity
- ✓ An Opportunity to Learn Something
- ✓ Developing Yourself
- ✓ Nuggets

Chapter Nine: Pushing Through Adversity
- ✓ Don't Stop, Time is Still Moving
- ✓ You will win if You Don't Quit

- ✓ Nuggets

Chapter Ten: Overnight Success Is a Myth
- ✓ Hard Work: The Mother of Success
- ✓ It's Too Early to Retire
- ✓ Conclusion
- ✓ Nuggets

Dedication

This book is dedicated to anyone going through any form of adversity

Foreword

A Nigerian sage once referred to adversity as the best teacher. In reality, the hard lessons of life are best learned by bitter experience. This, I believe, is the very essence and message of Bisi's expose in this lucid literature.

The writer Mrs. Bisi Osundeko happens to be my daughter, friend, and confidant all rolled into one. Having painstakingly gone through the manuscript, I feel honored to put down a few observations and comments.

The different vicissitudes of life have a divine purpose. A man's total outlook comprises nature and nurture, with the genes of the latter being rather suggestive. This means that they are themselves, products of a learning process. This exactly is where the hard lessons of life play a dominant role in molding the eventual character.

Thousands of examples abound since days of yore, viz:

•	The Three hundred brave Spartans who successfully stood against the mighty Persian army in 480B.C in the narrow Thermopylae.

•	The legendary Sir Winston Leonard Spencer Churchill, the heroic World War II British Prime Minister. Against all odds and in the face of the disaster of an invading formidable enemy, he mobilized all resources, exhibited ingenious statesmanship, and eventually turned imminent defeat to astounding victory.

•	The one hundred Pioneer Pilgrims Fathers who in 1620 left the comfort of England, crossed the mighty Atlantic Ocean in a wooden ship, the Mayflower, and founded modern-day North America.

•	Sir Francis Drake, Christopher Columbus, Marco Polo, the Spaniard explorers, and a host of others who all left their comfort zones and ventured in hitherto unknown lands.

•	The irrepressible lady Malala of Pakistan. Mahatma Gandhi of India, Mao Tse Tung of

China, and Joseph Stalin of the Soviet Union. Colonel Sanders of KFC fame.

All these heroes and heroines have something in common; an indomitable fighting spirit even in the face of daunting and seeming insurmountable disasters and monstrous problems. Such problems as would completely run down ordinary mortals.

Bisi's life experiences, for which she wasn't prepared, having lived a smooth and protected life, molded her personality. Her experiences are worth sharing as thousands would benefit from this. Her personality can be called a product of two worlds. In Nigeria the land of her birth, cultural practices dictate a resignation to voodoo and strange spiritual forces as being responsible for both good and bad fortunes. This is a world of witches, wizards, soothsayers, prophets, mullahs, and marabouts, where cult houses, shrines, mosques, and churches all constitute the most thriving industry. The average Nigerian would rather take recourse these institutions for daunting health or business problem, than face these lifetime normal challenges head-on.

The approach of the western world to solving life's problems is more pragmatic, being a system that evolved over several centuries. This is a product of the influx of cultures all over the entire world, with the varied experiences of nations that faced nature itself, the cosmos, the elements, wars, upheavals, disasters, epidemics, invasions, famine and recently COVID 19 stoically and with a stubborn resolve for survival and astounding success. With her exposure to this western culture over two decades, Bisi has benefited tremendously from a second learning process that has built her stoic and pragmatic personality.

As a published book, Bisi's thoughts will benefit thousands of readers going through their personal experiences of life. This makes this book a great gift for posterity.

-Engineer Lateef Banwo

Introduction

I have always been asked by lots and lots of people, especially clients, customers, people I come in contact with, people I mentor and there's always this question, even up to recently as well, that how do I manage to do so much because if it was somebody else, they would have likely broken down. I am asked how I manage to achieve balance; how do I manage to stay successful. When they then go on to find out that I am a mum to two children who have special needs, there is often this surprise, there is always this question: "How do you do it"?

For so long, I have been looking for the perfect opportunity to share my ideas as regards how I got here, how I have managed to build my business in the face of challenges, how I have remained successful, and the strategies that have helped me. Even though every individual in business is going to have individual challenges, there are some core strategies that I believe might work for another entrepreneur and person. Even if you don't have kids with special needs like me, there are some core principles that I have practiced over and over again that worked for me and I feel they would be useful to you too.

I, therefore, welcome you on a journey to discovering the principles of success amid adversity. See you at the top!

Chapter One

Adversity Is Part of Life

Chapter One
Adversity Is Part of Life

The man who fears adversity will never grow and he who abhors challenges may as well create his own cosmos. For as long as we live on this planet we must brace ourselves up for adversities. We live in a world of adversities, a world of storms, troubles, difficulties, and challenges. From the day we are born until the day we die, we would constantly come in contact with adversity and face difficult situations. A man that is born of a woman is of few days and full of troubles says the holy book. A child comes into this world squeezing itself through the cervical canal of its mother and experiencing for the first time such a crushing and excruciating pain as it journeys into a world of which it knows nothing. Before the doctors would say, Jack, the cry of a baby is heard, a new life is born and it is thanks to adversity. It is almost impossible to bring a new life into this world without some painful, difficult, and challenging processes. It is as though the difficulty that surrounds the birthing process is to prepare us for a world of adversity.

However, we grow up to detest adversity and forget too soon that we exist thanks to it. We humans do not always seem to remember that, had it not been for adversity, the process of our birth would not have been possible. So the question is "why do we come into this world through such a painful and adverse experience? The answer is simple! We live in a world of adversity and must of necessity be prepared and introduced to it at birth.

While I hold the above assertion to be true, I, however, want to say that the majority of people on earth today are afraid of adversity and see adversity as a curse. Many pray against adversity, some are sad to hear that word and others are conquered and defeated by it.

While it is true that people often shrink away from adversity, difficulties and life's challenges, and often wish that life is completely void of them, I, nevertheless, want

to assert that whether we like it or not, adversity is part of life and that everyone will at some point in their lives have a share of it whether in their businesses or daily life.
It doesn't matter our financial status, political affiliation, religion, race, or nationality, we would one day come face to face with adversity and the earlier we realize that and prepare for it, the much easier we would be able to handle and overcome it when it comes. It does not matter how much control you have over your finances, career, family, etc, you will agree with me that you do not have control over everything that happens to you in life. Adversity often takes us by surprise and when it hits, we have little or no control over it. That is why we must all evolve a mindset that sees adversity as part of life and as something inevitable and uncontrollable.
Cultivating the mindset that accepts that no matter how superhuman we are, we would not have control over everything, is key to overcoming adversity and challenges. Until I realized this truth, I could not overcome adversity. Yes! I had many adversities that

would have hindered my success and prevented me from fulfilling my life's dreams. I was able to overcome all my adversities because I got to a point in my life where I had to admit that adversity is part of life and that whether now or later every one of us would inevitably come to our place of adversity, we would all encounter adversity.

In the subsequent pages of this book, I am going to show you how accepting that adversity is normal and part of life helped me achieve a lot of success in my entrepreneurial journey and life. No one has achieved anything of worth that has not first encountered and overcome adversity.

"Show me someone who has done something worthwhile, and I'll show you someone who has overcome adversity."
– Lou Holtz

Before 2007, before my daughter was born, I, just like everyone else hated adversity and prayed that it never happened to me. I thought that it was abnormal to have adversity and one probably would have done something wrong to suffer adversity. Guess what! I was wrong. I was awoken to a rude shock on the day my daughter was born as we were told by the doctors that she was not going to be able to talk, walk, or do many other things that other children do. That was the day adversity knocked on my door and came into my life uninvited.

As I was trying to manage the difficulties and challenges that come with nurturing my daughter with special needs, I thought that was the first and last major adversity I would face in my life. Again, I was wrong. Fast forward two years later, my son was born and guess what! He was also born with a disability.

As a parent of two children with special needs, I have learned that adversity is part of life and we must get used to it. We must all get ready to accept adversity and prepare ourselves to live with adversity, love adversity, befriend adversity, and overcome adversity.

It was after I started accepting adversity as part of life and began to befriend it instead of running away from it that I developed the courage and skills to overcome it and succeed despite it. The common attitude with people who face adversity is to lament, blame others, and live in self-defeat. They think that the world is over and that nothing good could proceed out of their lives. If you have such an attitude, you will never overcome adversity. However, if you like me, accept adversity as part of life and befriend it, you would overcome it and succeed despite it. As long as you believe that troubles, challenges, and difficulties mean the end of the road for you, you would never develop the necessary traits for overcoming them. To overcome adversity, you must change your mindset and build your character until you become indomitable.

Building a Mindset and Character Development

If there is anything long-lasting that we gain from facing challenges and encountering adversity, it is the fact that adversity enables us to build a new mindset and develop character. Although our characters are determined by genes, they are also influenced by our environments and life's experiences such as challenges, adversity, and prior circumstances. Such character traits eventually become the strong foundation upon which we build successful businesses and life's endeavors.

You do not know exactly what you are capable of until you meet adversity. You know only a little or nothing about your strength if you have not been faced with challenges. Through adversity, we build our muscles, our strength, our skills, and our ability to succeed in life. When a sportsman goes to the gym to build his biceps muscles, he does that only by applying pressure, carrying heavy weighted metals, and overcoming difficulties. It does not matter how well he desires to build those muscles, if he doesn't intentionally bring himself to the gym and intentionally try to overcome adversity, heavyweights and difficult forces, he would never develop those muscles. The same is true with life and business and career. It doesn't matter how much you desire success and excellence in life, if you don't encounter adversity, you would rarely be able to develop the traits and skills that you need to succeed. Adversity, therefore, is a character builder. It molds you and prepares you for the journey of life. Challenges and difficulties of life are the fire that purifies you like gold and makes you more valuable and ready for excellence and success in all areas of your life.

He knows not his own strength that hath not met adversity.
-Cesare Pavese

Maybe you are currently facing one challenge or the other in your life and are thinking all your troubles would overwhelm you and that you would never survive these difficult times, I want you to understand that you could either turn this difficult time into the best season of your life or make it the worst. How can you turn difficult times into the best times? You do that by changing your mindset and allowing your circumstance to bring out the strength in you. Instead of lamenting and giving up on yourself, you should rather see your circumstance as an opportunity to grow, to become stronger, to learn, and to become better. You know not how strong you are until you have encountered adversity. The character traits that I cultivated thanks to being the mother of two kids with special needs eventually became the strong foundation upon which I built a successful business and life's career.

"As with the butterfly, adversity is necessary to build character in people."
– Joseph B. Wirthlin

Thanks to adversity, I developed a range of problem-solving skills, and some of those skills that I picked up in my journey as a special needs parent were translated into the skills that I am using to mentor other parents and business owners today. Those skills are also beneficial to me now that I am a politician.

Perhaps you are a special needs parent or an entrepreneur going through your own adversity this season and might be overburdened or feeling weighed down by the nature of challenges you might be experiencing. I want you to know that a lot of positive things can come out of facing adversity or challenges in your special needs parenting journey or your entrepreneurial life. I mentioned these aspects of life because the adversities that come with being a special needs parent and an entrepreneur are the things that have helped me succeed in life. The traits and mindset I developed along the way have become part and parcel of my life.

You may want to ask "why adversity? Why can't we live a life void of challenges?" Well, the answer is simple; life would be incomplete without adversity. We would never discover our strengths without adversity. I want you to realize that adversity has a lot of advantages and I will outline three of such advantages here. Until we understand these advantages we would have a hard time handling adversity.

1. Adversity helps us develop a range of problem-solving skills that are helpful in other areas of our lives.

2. Adversity helps us discover our true strength

"One who gains strength by overcoming obstacles possesses the only strength which can overcome adversity."
— Albert Schweitzer

3. Adversity often points us to our life's purpose and calling.

"Challenge and adversity are meant to help you know who you are. Storms hit your weakness, but unlock your true strength."
— Roy T. Bennett

Focusing on Time and Impact

One common mistake that people often make is to focus on their problems and calamities. They allow the thoughts of the challenges they are going through occupy their minds all day long. This is a huge error. If you focus on your problems and challenges, they would overwhelm you, incapacitate you and defeat you. Adversity ought not to rule your life and decide what you do or do not do. If you allow adversity to rule your life, you would only be reacting to circumstances instead of living a well-thought-out life. Successful people do not live reacting to life circumstances, they already know that life is full of challenges and are prepared to fulfill their dreams, achieve their goals and accomplish their life's purpose despite the adversities of life. That is why you must rather focus on your goals, dreams, and life's purpose instead of focusing on your circumstances. The fact that you have one adversity or the other should not prevent you from attending to other areas of your life that actually define you. Your challenges do not define you. You are not your circumstances. You have a life, a dream, a goal, an ambition to achieve before the unfortunate incidence or circumstance happened. Are you going to sacrifice all of that and trade it all for adversity? Are you going to abandon that dream, that ambition, that career, that purpose all because you are facing a challenge in one area of your life? No, you would not do that. If you want to live an impactful and successful life, you must focus on the proper use of time to create a lasting impact in the lives of others and society at large instead of focusing on your challenges and adversities. Time is too precious to be wasted focusing on the things that we cannot change and have no control over. You have just one life to live and you do not want to waste it lamenting about your challenges when you could invest it creating impact in your community and nation.

Despite my adversities, I chose to become successful and impactful. People wonder how I am able to succeed in business and career despite my circumstances. They wonder how I am able to be so impactful to the extent that I won several awards. My answer is simple. It is "focus" I decided to focus on how I could use my time to achieve the things I can control instead of wasting my time lamenting on the things I can't control. My focus is completely different from what people want me to focus on. Now I am a lot more even aware of my time and mortality, of the fact that whether or not I have children with disabilities, I would someday exit this earth. So, I look at life as finite and understand the fact that I have a certain amount of time which I don't know on earth. How am I going to use that time? How am I going to impact the lives of others? Of course, starting with my family, how am I going to be the best mum to my children?: The best wife to my husband? How am I going to be the best version of myself daily so that whenever God calls me home, I can say that "Yes! I fulfilled my purpose, I actualized my dreams and I changed the world for good. Adversity is not meant to terminate your purpose and life goals but to strengthen and prepare you for your life's journey. Successful people succeed and fulfill their dreams, ambitions, and purpose against all odds. Such was the like of Helen Keller. The name Helen Keller is known around the world as a symbol of courage in the face of overwhelming odds, yet she was much more than a symbol. She was a woman of luminous intelligence, high ambition, and great accomplishment who devoted her life to helping others.[1]

Hellen Keller was faced with adversity from childhood and throughout her entire life. When she was only a few months old as a child, she lost her sight and hearing due to a mysterious fever. She, however, did not allow her adversity to limit her life's goals and ambitions. She focused on purpose, ambition, and success instead of focusing on her challenges like most people erroneously do. With such determination to succeed, she overcame her deafness and blindness to become a strong, educated woman who spoke about and promoted women's rights.[2]

That is how everyone should face adversity; with the belief that despite our adversities we can succeed and impact the world positively.

How Adversity Changed My Life

It is not only true that adversity is part of life but also that it changes our lives. No matter how well we've planned our lives, when adversity comes, it alters everything. For me, I had set out a perfect life before me. I had plans of how I thought my life should go, and how I was going to have my kids at a young age. So, because I had set these plans in my head – plans which I thought defined a perfect life, I was not anticipating any adversity. I was barely 26 when I had my daughter and all through my nine months of pregnancy, there was no indication at all that my daughter was going to be born with a disability. I was so sure that I wasn't that sort of person that could have a child with a disability. I believed in myself so much so that I thought the prenatal tests that I was supposed to do were not necessary. I just boastfully said to the nurse "look, I am below 30 and I have read during my university days about genetics and understood that a child with Down syndrome cannot be born to a woman who is under 30years of age". I was so sure that I was immune to certain things. Unfortunately for me, I didn't know that adversity is not a respecter of persons and that we all no matter how perfect we think we are would at some point and in some areas of our lives experience our share of adversity.

When my daughter was born, she was born with Down syndrome. I could not believe my eyes. The very area of my life where I least expected a challenge was where my adversity came from. The very medical possibility which I thought I was immune to was the very condition that led to my adversity. Giving birth to a child with a complex array of disabilities was a major life even that sort of shook me to the core. It changed my mindset and my entire life. Everything I thought I had planned out about my future that made me think my life would be a bed of roses suddenly became like a mirage to me. I have always had everything I wanted, come to be as planned. I am the sort of person that would just get a pen and say, "before this age or that age, I want to achieve this or that. Because I am a very hard working person, my plans get executed and happen the way I had planned them. That was why I wasn't surprised when in secondary school I was the second overall best student in the whole of Lagos State in the exams – Junior West Africa Examination Council (WAEC) examination. Then in my General School Certificate Examination (GCE), my result was also the best in the whole of the center. Then even before having my daughter at that point, I was on my master's program and I was on a scholarship, and the scholarship I won was only given to 10 people in the world.

So, I have had a smooth life before adversity hit. You know what it means to just have life going the way you planned it! You just go through life when you've had that sort of privilege, where you read, download everything, and are constantly used to having things work. So, you just go through life sailing as if whatever you set your heart to get you get. That was why on that particular day my daughter was born, one of the things that went through my head was, "oh my God! Oh my God! I didn't plan for this! I didn't plan for this!" "What do I do?" "How am I going to help her?" "Down syndrome comes with a learning disability, wheelchair, etc. "what am I going to do?" "Oh! my God! Oh! My God! All through these nine months I have already started a plan of how I am sort of going to build her life but I haven't got plans for this special needs parenting, I hadn't read any books about being a parent of a child with special needs. I just felt so unprepared and I was like "oh my God!" and this is the issue with being used to having things work for you, constantly thinking that well, as long as you are hardworking, good, diligent, everything has to fall in place. But then a whole new chapter opened up to me, I had become a nurturer, a caregiver and a mother to a vulnerable child who even holding her felt like a rag doll due to her hypotonia(low muscle tone). I said to myself "actually, I have no clue what I am going to do from here" at that particular point. From that point till now, it has been a journey, building my business into one of the biggest babywearing brands in the United Kingdom. It has been a journey, redefining what success meant to me. It isn't just about acquiring good grades or awards, it is about getting prepared for good and bad times. Life could happen to you at any point and change all your plans, so be ready! Although adversity changed my life, I was still able to conquer it and succeed. One thing that has been very helpful for me is building my mindset and developing character. In times of adversity, it takes a lot of strength to reach a point in your life where you are no longer afraid of adversity and being realistic about the fact that adversity is a part of life.

So actually accepting the fact that adversity does not mean that you are a failure. Changing your mindset will help you to achieve success. Understanding that you are not going to have absolute control over every single challenge but they would be challenges that you will have control over and then you will need practice with time, to be able to identify which ones you have control over. You will be able to develop problem-solving skills and that is something that has helped me in life. So it is really important for us not to run away from challenges but for us to see it as a stepping stone to success. There is always something to learn at every point in time from adversity.

Nuggets One

1. The man who fears adversity will never grow and he who abhors challenges may as well create his own cosmos. For as long as we live on this planet we must brace ourselves up for adversities

2. It is almost impossible to bring a new life into this world without some painful, difficult, and challenging processes. It is as though the difficulty that surrounds the birthing process is to prepare us for a world of adversity.

3. It doesn't matter our financial status, political affiliation, religion, race, or nationality, we would one day come face to face with adversity and the earlier we realize that and prepare for it, the much easier we would be able to handle and overcome it when it comes.

4. No one has achieved anything of worth that has not first encountered and overcome adversity.

5. As long as you believe that troubles, challenges, and difficulties mean the end of the road for you, you would never develop the necessary traits for overcoming them. To overcome adversity, you must change your mindset and build your character until you become indomitable.

6. You do not know exactly what you are capable of until you meet adversity. You know only a little or nothing about your strength if you have not been faced with challenges. Through adversity, we build our muscles, our strength, our skills, and our ability to succeed in life.

7. It doesn't matter how much you desire success and excellence in life, if you don't encounter adversity, you would rarely be able to develop the traits and skills that you need to succeed.

8. Adversity is a character builder. It molds you and prepares you for the journey of life.

9. Challenges and difficulties of life are the fire that purifies you like gold and makes you more valuable and ready for excellence and success in all areas of your life.
10. If you allow adversity to rule your life, you would only be reacting to circumstances instead of living a well-thought-out life. Successful people do not live reacting to life circumstances, they already know that life is full of challenges and are prepared to fulfill their dreams, achieve their goals and accomplish their life's purpose despite the adversities of life.

Chapter Two

Attitude Is Everything

Chapter Two
Attitude Is Everything

In the previous chapter, we discussed the need to accept adversity as being part of life and how that can help make the process of overcoming adversity much easier. In this chapter, we shall discuss how maintaining a positive attitude in times of crisis and adversity gives us the strength to overcome and succeed.

Maintaining a Positive Attitude

While most people lament, lose faith, give up and resort to a life of self-pity and mediocrity in times of adversity, I have learned from experience that none of such actions aid our recovery, healing, and winning process. They rather cripple us more and incapacitate us. The secret to overcoming adversity is having the right mental attitude. You could either be defeated by adversity or overcome adversity.

The difference is in your attitude. The question is not whether or not you will experience adversity in your life, we all will. The question is what will you do when adversity comes? How will you respond to adversity? Adversity could propel you in the direction of your destiny or hinder you from reaching that destiny; the direction you go depends on your attitude to adversity.

The same wind blows on us all; the winds of disaster, opportunity and change. Therefore, it is not the blowing of the wind, but the setting of the sails that will determine our direction in life.
-Jim Rohn

Your attitude to adversity sets the sail in your life's journey. The effect adversity has on our life and business is dependent on our attitude to it. Maintaining a positive attitude in times of adversity is a key factor in overcoming adversity and building a successful business and life nevertheless.

Successful people defy unimaginable personal odds, obstacles, and adversities to achieve their success but mediocre people faint and give up at the slightest challenge they encounter. Little wonder there are more mediocre people than successful people in the world. The reason the rich and successful make-up only a small percentage of the world's population compared to the poor is that only a few people can cultivate enough positive attitude to succeed amidst difficulties and calamities.

Isaac Lidsky was one such successful people who despite being faced with adversities, cultivated enough positive attitude to succeed nonetheless.

Isaac Lidsky was diagnosed at age 13 with a condition that completely robbed him of his sight by age 25. He was initially thought that he would never succeed in life and business because of his adversity.

"Initially, I was depressed and terrified," Lidsky told Business News Daily. "I had preconceived misconceptions about disabilities and limitations, and I felt helpless. Family, friends, and several angels in my life helped me to develop the vision to overcome blindness as I lost my sight."

Though his vision was failing, Lidsky graduated from Harvard College before he turned 20, founded and sold a tech company, and earned a law degree that landed him a job as a Department of Justice lawyer.

Today, Lidksy serves as the CEO of home building company ODC Construction, which has built tens of thousands of Florida homes, and which brought in more than $68 million in gross revenue last year. When asked how he was able to achieve such feats despite his disability, Lidsky said his business success is a result of his ability to let go of his internal fears and take control of his situation.

"I had mental images about blindness and the limitations it would impose upon me and my ability to achieve," he said. "I discovered that those mental images were self-limiting fiction, not a natural truth about the world.

"At the same time, I learned that the ultimate responsibility for my life and my limitations begins and ends with me," Lidsky continued. "It is my responsibility to proactively identify obstacles in my way and to look for solutions. There is no limit to the human ability to adapt or the human imagination to create. There are practical solutions for discrete challenges. It is our responsibility to find them and use them to accomplish what we decide to achieve for ourselves."[1]

Who said you cannot overcome your adversity and succeed in your business and career? Who said that adversity is the end of the road for you? Having suffered adversity myself, I can boldly tell you that our adversities do not determine our success as much as our attitude to those adversities does. If you can maintain a positive attitude amid adversity, you are already on your way to overcoming that adversity.

If you have a positive attitude and constantly strive to give your best effort, eventually you will overcome your immediate problems and find you are ready for greater challenges.
-Pat Riley

Achieving a positive mental attitude both in business life and family takes practice, and doesn't just happen suddenly. One has to consciously cultivate a positive attitude if one must overcome adversity and become successful in life and business.

This is a particular aspect of my life that I have had to work on gradually. I don't think anybody can simply just arrive at or achieve a positive attitude straight away in one goal or one day while pursuing success in business and daily life. No, that is possibly the social media view of entrepreneurship, that you start your business today and then the next day everything just booms. No, it has been a journey. Achieving a positive mental attitude both in my business life and family has taken practice, it has been a journey, and it involves a deliberate growth process.

Never give up
The reason most people fail in life and allow themselves to be defeated by adversity is their inability to keep on going in the direction of their dreams once they come in contact with obstacles or distracting challenges. If we must

overcome adversity and win over life's challenges, we must learn to never give up or bow down to difficult circumstances. Most people fail in life not because they could not have subdued their adversities and challenges but because they gave up too quickly and easily. History is replete with stories of great people who overcame adversity and achieved success simply because they refused to give up on their dreams, goals, and ambitions in the face of adversity.

Though it might sound like a cliché that successful business owners like me always advise others never to give up, the truth however is that this is the core strategy that I have used to succeed amid numerous adversities. The principle of "never give up" has worked for me and many other successful entrepreneurs and great achievers. It is a fact that there will be so many reasons for you as a business owner to want to give up, but if you do not quit, you will succeed.

Never give up, for that is just the place and time that the tide will turn."
—Harriet Beecher Stowe

Tyler Perry is a very popular name in the movie industry. He is the first African-American to own a major film and TV studio. Today, he is a writer, actor, director, and movie producer with a net worth of about $600 million. How did he become such a successful entrepreneur? Was the process without challenges? No! Perry's success was born out of adversity. He had a rough childhood and had he given up on his dreams, he would probably not be known by anyone today. He was physically and sexually abused growing up, got kicked out of high school, and tried to commit suicide twice—once as a preteen and again at 22. At 23, he moved to Atlanta and took up odd jobs as he started working on his stage career.

In 1992, he wrote, produced, and starred in his first theater production, I Know I've Been Changed, somewhat informed by his difficult upbringing. Perry put all his savings into the show and it failed miserably; the run lasted just one weekend and only 30 people came to watch. He kept up with the production, working more odd jobs, and often slept in his car to get by. Six years later, Perry finally broke through when, on its seventh run, the show became a success. He's since gone on to have an extremely successful career as a director, writer, and actor. Perry was named Forbes' highest-paid man in entertainment in 2011.[2]

How do you explain such success in the face of adversity without attributing it to one thing "the never give up" spirit! The never-give-up attitude is the secret to all successes that happen amidst setbacks, obstacles, and adversity. Until a man cultivates such a never-give-up attitude, he is not yet ready to succeed. The road to success is full of obstacles and only those who have resolved to surmount obstacles and journey through adversity to their destination truly succeed. The rest, the mediocre lot, the weak-spirited fall by the way and give up on their dreams. The reason successful people don't give up in the face of adversity is that they have learned to maintain a positive attitude amid setbacks.

"Keep Going, Your hardest times often lead to the greatest moments of your life. Keep going. Tough situations build strong people in the end."
― Roy T. Bennett

Maintaining a positive attitude also involves learning from failure. I learned from failure how to never give up and how to succeed. Before setting up my current business, Joy and Joe Limited, I was into some other businesses that did not succeed as I thought. For some reasons those businesses flopped. The truth is that whether you like it or not there will be so many reasons for you as a business owner to want to give up and then if you are a special needs parent like me, you will face huge challenges that will affect your ability to be able to juggle multiple responsibilities. Challenges like how to get your children to hospitals occasionally when they have hospital appointments, random and unexpected ailments, etc. can show up and obstruct your schedule and routine. Your child might be well today and then the next day he or she has a cough that just gets out of hand. The challenges that come with raising special needs children and being an entrepreneur are many but the goal of this book is to teach you how to succeed despite any challenges. So, how does one succeed despite huge challenges? The answer lies in, firstly developing one's mind and cultivating a positive attitude. That is why I work on my mind, working on myself gradually, and learning by feeding my mind with the right and positive information. The second secret to succeeding amid numerous challenges and setbacks is to learn from your mistakes and failures. Those challenges are there not to destroy you but to teach you.

Failure is A Teacher

Have you ever suffered adversity in business or any area of your life? Have you ever failed, trying to achieve a goal? If your answer is yes, then I want you to know that you are not alone. You are in good company. I have not known any extremely successful entrepreneur who hasn't failed before. The only people who do not fail are those who do not try anything. They spend their entire life in mediocrity because they are too timid to try anything for fear that they might fail. Successful people, however, take the bold steps, dare failure in the face, fail, learn their lessons, and try again until they succeed. For such people, success usually comes to them in huge amounts as a result of their huge experience with failure and the wealth of knowledge they have accrued learning from failure. I didn't become a successful entrepreneur overnight. I actually learned from failure. I am successful today because there was a time when failure became my teacher. Learning from things that haven't worked in some of my past businesses and seeing how I can do them better and constantly trying to outdo anything I have done in the past is the reason I can tell my success story today. If success were easy, there would be no poor and mediocre people in our world today. We would all be successful if success comes on a platter of gold. Unfortunately, it doesn't! It comes through years of failure and hard work. Years of learning from failure leads to success.

Jack Ma failed a key primary school test two times, failed the middle school test three times, failed the college entrance exam two times, and yet never gave up. He applied to Harvard ten times and was rejected all ten times yet he never gave up. After graduating from college, he applied to 30 different jobs and was subsequently rejected by all of them. He even applied to be a police officer. But they didn't even give him the time of day,rejecting him with three simple words: "You're no good." Later on, he applied to work for KFC but out of the 24 applicants, Ma was the only one that was rejected. The rest were hired.[3]

Eventually, Ma created an online marketplace called Alibaba which has become one of the most popular online marketplaces in the world. Today, Jack Ma is among the richest people in the world with a net worth of about 44 billion USD (2020). His success story and that of many others like him is proof that becoming a successful entrepreneur is possible irrespective of the numerous adversities that life throws at us. If we don't give up, we would succeed in the end. We may indeed fail sometimes, but to succeed in life, we must learn from failure and never see failure as a negative thing but an opportunity to learn and become better.

Failure is a great teacher, and I think when you make mistakes and you recover from them and you treat them as valuable learning experiences, then you've got something to share.
-Steve Harvey

Learning from failure and not seeing failure as a full stop helped me on my journey to success. Experience has shown me that success will never be easy to achieve and the earlier you realize that the better for you. You'll face adversities, setbacks, and challenges whether you like it or not. The rest is up to you! Are you going to let adversity defeat you or you are going to develop the attitude of a winner and refuse to give up? Remember that no matter what happens, the future is beautiful if you don't quit!

"Today is cruel. Tomorrow is crueler. And the day after tomorrow is beautiful."
-Jack Ma

Nuggets Two

1. The secret to overcoming adversity is having the right mental attitude. You could either be defeated by adversity or overcome adversity. The difference is in your attitude.
2. Maintaining a positive attitude in times of adversity is a key factor in overcoming adversity and building a successful business and life nevertheless.
3. Successful people defy unimaginable personal odds, obstacles, and adversities to achieve their success but mediocre people faint and give up at the slightest challenge they encounter.
4. The reason the rich and successful make-up only a small percentage of the world's population compared to the poor is that only a few people can cultivate enough positive attitude to succeed amidst difficulties and calamities.
5. Our adversities do not determine our success as much as our attitude to those

adversities does. If you can maintain a positive attitude amid adversity, you are already on your way to overcoming that adversity.

6. The reason most people fail in life and allow themselves to be defeated by adversity is their inability to keep on going in the direction of their dreams once they come in contact with obstacles or distracting challenges.
7. Most people fail in life not because they could not have subdued their adversities and challenges but because they gave up too quickly and easily.
8. The secret to succeeding amid numerous challenges and setbacks is to learn from your mistakes and failures. Those challenges are there not to destroy you but to teach you.
9. The only people who do not fail are those who do not try anything. They spend their entire life in mediocrity because they are too timid to try anything for fear that they might fail. Successful people, however, take

the bold steps, dare failure in the face, fail, learn their lessons, and try again until they succeed.
10.   If success were easy, there would be no poor and mediocre people in our world today. We would all be successful if success comes on a platter of gold. Unfortunately, it doesn't! It comes through years of failure and hard work. Years of learning from failure lead to success.

Chapter Three
Knowing Your Why

In the previous chapter, we discussed why having the right attitude is instrumental in overcoming adversity. In this chapter, we shall discuss how the knowledge of your original motive and clarity of purpose aid the process of overcoming adversity.

Why Do You Do What You Do?

Do you know why a lot of people abandon their dreams and ambitions and give up on life in general during their season of adversity? While there may be a couple of reasons that happens, I however want to focus on one of them which I think is paramount and it has to do with purpose. Yes! Purpose! The reason a lot of people fail and give up in times of adversity is a lack of clarity of purpose. While it is true that we all face challenges and difficult circumstances, those who know the why behind their dreams and ambitions focus on it and stay motivated to succeed despite the adversity that surrounds them. For those who have no clear purpose and reason behind their pursuit of life's endeavors, adversity means stop. To them, they see adversity as a "stop signal" and interpret every setback to mean "give up! You can't make it!"

The difference between successful people and mediocre people is simply the presence or absence of a clear purpose. When you know the why behind that business, that career goal, that ambition, and that dream, you would defy all setbacks and adversities to pursue it. The reason people give up on their dreams in times of adversity is not really because they could not have overcome adversity and succeeded but because they do not know why they had those dreams in the first place. If you were sailing in a ship to a destination where you would on arrival be the only hope to rescuing a group of school children among whom are your two beloved kids from death, would you give up on the journey and turn back when the waves of the sea ahead of you become boisterous or you would defy the wind of adversity and journey on. I guess your answer would be to press on, to keep sailing and looking for the best direction to beat the winds. Why is that so? Why would you want to dare the storm and keep sailing despite it? The reason is simple; clarity of purpose and beyond that, the worthiness of purpose. The fact that you know in clear terms why you started that journey and how important that "why" is, gives you the courage and motivation to keep sailing amidst the winds of adversity that try to hamper your journey. Now imagine if you were in that ship because a friend invited you to just come along without a clear understanding of why or what to do on arrival. Would you desire to risk your life when the storm hits or you would beg to stop the journey and return home? I guess you wouldn't want to risk your life for a no-worthy-cause. Nobody would!

So, why did I give you those scenarios? It is because I want you to view life in such a perspective; one that considers every action in terms of purpose and value. Why do you do the things that you do? Why did you start that business, that career, job, educational pursuit, that non-profit organization etc? Your answer to these questions would determine whether or not you would give up when adversity hits any of these endeavors. When you face setbacks and challenges in life, understanding your "why" becomes the only motivation that keeps you going. To overcome the adversities of life, we must understand the reason we exist and are pursuing the dreams and ambitions that we pursue.

One reason I became a successful entrepreneur and politician despite being a mother to special needs children is the understanding of my why and the purpose of my being.
 The secret of my success in the face of adversity is clarity of purpose and a constant reminder of my original motive.
My "why" is my motive! Knowing my motive has been one of the core principles that helped me as a mum to two children with special needs to be able to create a successful business and life. Knowing my "why" is understanding the reasons I am doing what I am doing and it is quite a coincidence that my business is an eponymous business named Joy and Joe baby

slings– has the names of my two children – so there is always a constant reminder that something is motivating me to do this.

Remember Your Original Motive

Overcoming adversity has so much to do with understanding why you do what you do and allowing that "why" to motivate you daily. In addition to that, if you could clarify your vision and write it down as a constant reminder, you would be able to thrive in life and business irrespective of the challenges and difficult circumstances that may plague your life. Remembering your "why" – the reason you are doing that business, that career, or whatever dream you are chasing will help you overcome your adversity and keep you going forward in the direction of success. It is like fuel in a car. If your car lacks fuel you will not be able to move. Always remember your why and you would more easily overcome adversity and succeed in life.

For me, there is always a constant motivation and that has to do with having my children's names behind my business brand. Seeing the name of my children on the brand is a constant motivation and even just thinking about my children has been inspirational to me. They inspire me all the time and I draw strength and the courage to succeed from them as well. The desire to constantly want to be the best mum I can push me to work harder and do everything I can do to succeed. Knowing my "why" is having the motive behind what I do. So when setbacks and challenges come, the motive behind why I do what I do becomes the fuel that keeps me going.

If you are a business owner, you would agree with me that there would be tough times, times when your competition will get out of control and almost kick you out of the market. There would be times when you might not be meeting your goals. The question is "what will you do at such a time?" It is common to see a lot of people give up in times like this. However, those who have a strong motivation, who know why they started the journey in the first place, would keep going in the direction of their dreams no matter what happens. Without a clear original motive, people give up on their dreams and ambitions. But those who know why they do what they do would defy all setbacks, adversities, and challenges and go ahead to become successful.

Write the Vision and Make It Plain

Having a core motive behind your mind about your business or career pursuit is a huge advantage as it will help you move courageously in the direction of your dreams no matter the amount of adversity that tries to stop you. However, to remember your original motive and not lose sight of it, you would need to write it down. That vision that you saw initially that prompted you to take that business step, that career step, that project, etc. ought to always be at close sight. You need to always rehearse that vision that got you started on the journey in the first place. Most people fail in times of adversity because they forget the vision they had at the beginning.

And without that vision in sight, there is no motivation to keep on going when calamity strikes. That is why you need to write down your vision somewhere so that you can always refer to it and allow it to be your inspiration as you journey through adversity to success. You might even just write it down in your office space or your bedroom. Make it visible and constantly recite it to yourself. When you wake up, let it be the first thing you see that reminds you of your "why" – your reason, your purpose, your motive.

Those who do not write down their vision soon forget it and when adversity comes, they surrender and get defeated by it. Because they lack vision or have forgotten their vision, they are void of hope and think that adversity is the end of the world for them. Vision gives hope in times of adversity, the lack of it leads to self-defeat.

"Where there is no vision, there is no hope."
-George Washington Carver

Having my vision written down and always before my eyes and in my mind is something that has always kept me going. It is like fuel in a car. Just the way your car will not be able to move if it lacks fuel, that is how you will not be able to progress in life if you lack vision especially in times of adversity. Your vision becomes your anchor in times of adversity, setbacks, and challenges. It is the drive you need to continue working hard, persevering, and believing that someday, you will arrive at your destiny, the place where visions are realized and dreams are fulfilled.

So, constantly just replenishing my mind and reminding myself of my vision and ambition gives me the strength to work harder and that is the strategy and secret to my success and achievements. You too can defy setbacks and limitations and succeed by writing down your visions and ambitions and relentlessly pursuing them.

In life, most people focus on their adversities and give up on life while others focus on their visions, ambitions, and cultivate hope and self-belief to achieve them. The outcome of your life in times of adversity depends on whether you are focusing on your adversity or your vision.

One of the most strategic secrets to overcoming adversities and life's challenges is to constantly gaze on the vision and dream for which you started whatever journey you are embarking on. Whether you like it or not, the road to destiny, success, and accomplishment is full of setbacks and bottlenecks. Whether or not you will arrive at your preferred destination amidst the numerous adversities is dependent largely on your ability to visualize your destination from where you currently are. You may be standing right now at a point in your life's journey where you are buffeted by all kinds of adversities, but you must visualize your destination; that original vision and dream that you had at the beginning of your journey. That is a sure way to overcoming adversities. If you must overcome adversity, you must so much want to succeed to the extent that you focus daily on your vision and let it inspire you amid your challenges. When you write down your vision and focus on it every day instead of your adversity, you energize yourself to live beyond that adversity into the reality of your dreams, goals, and ambitions. If you constantly see your original vision, purpose, and dreams, you would most likely achieve them, regardless of the setback that will try to hinder you.

Nuggets Three

1. The reason a lot of people fail and give up in times of adversity is a lack of clarity of purpose. While it is true that we all face challenges and difficult circumstances, those who know the why behind their dreams and ambitions focus on it and stay motivated to succeed despite the adversity that surrounds them.
2. The difference between successful people and mediocre people is simply the presence or absence of a clear purpose. When you know the why behind that business, that career goal, that ambition, and that dream, you would defy all setbacks and adversities to pursue it.
3. The reason people give up on their dreams in times of adversity is not really because they could not have overcome

adversity and succeeded but because they do not know why they had those dreams in the first place.
4. Overcoming adversity has so much to do with understanding why you do what you do and allowing that "why" to motivate you daily.
5. If you could clarify your vision and write it down as a constant reminder, you would be able to thrive in life and business irrespective of the challenges and difficult circumstances that may plague your life.
6. Without a clear original motive, people give up on their dreams and ambitions. But those who know why they do what they do would defy all setbacks, adversities, and challenges and go ahead to become successful.
7. Most people fail in times of adversity because they forget the vision they had at the beginning. And without that vision in sight, there is no motivation to keep on going when calamity strikes.

8. Vision gives hope in times of adversity, the lack of it leads to self-defeat.

9. Your vision becomes your anchor in times of adversity, setbacks, and challenges. It is the drive you need to continue working hard, persevering, and believing that someday, you will arrive at your destiny, the place where visions are realized and dreams fulfilled.

10. In life, most people focus on their adversities and give up on life while others focus on their visions, ambitions, and cultivate hope and self-belief to achieve them. The outcome of your life in times of adversity depends on whether you are focusing on your adversity or your vision.

Chapter Four

Your Association Matters

Chapter Four
Your Association Matters

In the previous chapter, we discussed the importance of knowing your "why" or the reason you do what you do as you journey through life. In this chapter, we shall discuss why the association you keep on your life's journey matters a lot and how that association affects you in times of adversity.

Surrounding Yourself with the Right People

The reason some people fail and give up in times of adversity is not really because they could not have overcome that adversity but because they listened to people who demoralized them and told them that they would never be able to succeed amid their storms. Many people surround themselves with dream killers and pessimistic people who talk them out of their dreams and ambitions in their times of difficulties.

The rise or fall, success or failure of your dreams is largely dependent on the association you build yourself around."
— *Israelmore Ayivor*

If you must overcome adversity and succeed in life, you must as a matter of necessity have the right association. The need to have the right association as a prerequisite to overcoming adversity and succeeding in business and life, in general, cannot be overemphasized. One strategy that has been quite useful for me and the reason I can succeed amidst my challenges is surrounding myself with the right people. I have learned over the years that, to build an exceptionally successful business and family life amid adversity requires that one surrounds oneself with the right people. This is so important and thankfully, my parenting journey has been the type that has kept me busy, positively busy such that there is no time on my hands to laze around with the wrong crowd. Keeping the right association is so important that the success or failure of your business, career, dreams, and ambitions depend on it. Whether you believe it or not, the association we keep goes a long way to affect our mindset and the decisions we take in times of challenges. You do not want to keep company with negative people especially in times of adversity; otherwise, you would be orchestrating your downfall and failure. The reason is that when you keep associating with negative people, you will only hear negativity and think negatively. Pessimism is a hindrance to determination, perseverance, and self-belief and the man who spends his time with pessimistic people is unknowingly heading for failure. Imagine being around people who say words like "you can't make it, you do not have what it takes to succeed, you will fail if you take the risk, this adversity will overwhelm you, or this mountain is insurmountable, etc." What do you think will happen to your life and business? Your life would be full of negative energy, self-doubt, fear, discouragement, and desperation.

Indeed, we will all go through one adversity or the other in our life's journey but when you keep company with people who are always pessimistic and complaining about their adversities, it will not be long before you will start being pessimistic and doubtful about your ability to succeed amid your difficulties. Your association matters a lot. You cannot be optimistic if you spend too much time with pessimistic people. You can't be positive when you are always in the company of negative people. It is difficult to walk forward in the company of people who are walking backward. One of the greatest secrets to overcoming adversity is to walk with people who encourage, inspire, and are going in the same direction as you.

Who is in Your Boat?

Why is the company you keep important and how does it affect your progress in life? It is important because you are influenced by the company you keep. The outcome of your life is hugely dependent on the association you keep. When it comes to relationships, we are greatly influenced — whether we like it or not — by those closest to us. It affects our way of thinking, our self-esteem, and our decisions. Of course, everyone is a unique person, but research has shown that we're more affected by our environment than we think.[1]

It was Jim Rohn who said that we are the average of the five people we spend most of our time with and I quite agree with him. Most of the traits we acquire in life come directly from the people that we spend most of our time with. This is the reason we must be careful in choosing the kind of people we surround ourselves with.

If we surround ourselves with lazy, visionless, and pessimistic people, they would discourage, impede, and hinder our progress. If we must overcome adversity, we need to associate with people who are optimistic, foresighted, and believe in our dreams. Whether we accept it or not, the kind of people that we interact within our time of challenges and difficulties will one way or the other influence us either positively or negatively. I always bear that in mind and always try my best as an entrepreneur and a special needs parent to have some sort of control over the kind of people that I surround me with. That has been one of my secrets of success despite my adversities.

I want to encourage you to be very selective in your choice of friends and people you allow to influence your life if you want to overcome adversity and live a successful life.

A man only learns in two ways, one by reading, and the other by association with smarter people.
-Will Rogers

From the day I understood the fact that we learn and become smarter by associating with smart, intelligent, and inspiring people, I resolved never to waste my time with demoralizing, inane, and lethargic people anymore. Why should I be in the company of people who kill hope, destroy initiatives and discourage dreams when I could spend the same time with people who encourage, inspire, and energize me to walk in the direction of my dreams!

Listen, dear friend, you cannot overcome adversity and succeed by keeping company with people who see impossibilities in every situation. It will almost be impossible for you to succeed in business and life in general if you surround yourself with negative people. You will not be able to maximize your full potential when all you see and hear every day is impossibilities and self-doubt.

Perhaps you are familiar with the popular story of the eagle that grew up amid chickens, and which because of wrong association could not maximize its potential to soar. This story is often used to explain the importance of choosing the right association. Here it is:

A long time ago in a remote valley, there lived a farmer. One day he was tired of the daily routine of running the farm and decided to climb the cliffs that brooded above the valley to see what lay beyond. He climbed all day until he reached a ledge just below the top of the cliff; there, to his amazement was a nest, full of eggs.

Immediately, he knew they were eagle's eggs. Even though he knew it was un-ecological and almost certainly illegal, he carefully took one and stowed it in his pack. Then seeing the sun was low in the sky, he realized it was too late in the day to make the top and slowly began to make his way down the cliff to his farm. When he got home he put the egg in with the few chickens he kept in the yard. The mother hen was the proudest chicken you ever saw, sitting atop this magnificent egg; and the cockerel could not have been prouder.

Sure enough, some weeks later, from the egg emerged a fine, healthy eaglet. Also, as is in the gentle nature of chickens, they did not balk at the stranger in their midst and raised the majestic bird as one of their own. Therefore, it was that the eagle grew up with its brother and sister chicks. It learned to do all the things chickens do: it clucked and cackled, scratching in the dirt for grits and worms, flapping its wings furiously, flying just a few feet in the air before crashing down to earth in a pile of dust and feathers.

It believed resolutely that it was a chicken. One day, late in its life, the eagle-who-thought-he-was-a-chicken happened to look up at the sky. High overhead, soaring majestically and effortlessly on the thermals with scarcely a single beat of its powerful golden wings was an eagle!

"What's that?" cried the old eagle in awe. "It's magnificent! So much power and grace! It's beautiful!"

"That's an eagle", replied a nearby chicken, "That's the King of the Birds. It is a bird of the air… not for the likes of us. We're only chickens; we're birds of the earth".

With that, they all cast their eyes downwards once more and continued digging in the dirt. Therefore, it was that the eagle lived and died a chicken… because that is all it believed itself to be.[2]

Why did I share this story with you? It is so that you can see how dangerous it is to keep the wrong company. Just like this eagle who thought it was a chicken, you would think that you cannot succeed, the courage to accomplish your goals, and the wisdom to solve your problems if you keep company with weak-minded people. You will begin to doubt your natural talents, skills, and shrewdness if you allow mediocre people to dictate what you can or can't do. In times of adversity, you need people that will push you in the direction of your dreams, people that can synergize your potential to overcome that adversity and those who believe in you. If you surround yourself with negative, mediocre, and weak people in times of adversity, you would hardly be able to overcome that adversity.

To overcome difficulties and life's challenges, you must believe in yourself and surround yourself with like-minded people who believe in you, in the possibility of your dreams and in your ability to succeed.

"You need to associate with people that inspire you, people that challenge you to rise higher, people that make you better. Don't waste your valuable time with people that are not adding to your growth. Your destiny is too important."
-Joel Osteen

As I begin to bring this chapter to a close, I want you to think about your closest company, the people in your boat. Do they inspire you to pursue your dreams, do they empower you to overcome your adversities, do they educate you on how to succeed in your business and career, and do they add value to your life? If your answer to these questions is "no", it is time you changed your company, it's high time you exited that association and go look for the right people. If you keep company with people who are against the direction of your sail, how would you get to your destination?

Nuggets Four

1. The reason some people fail and give up in times of adversity is not really because they could not have overcome that adversity but because they listened to people who demoralized them and told them that they would never be able to succeed amid their storms.
2. To build an exceptionally successful business and family life amid adversity requires that one surrounds oneself with the right people.
3. Whether you believe it or not, the association we keep goes a long way to affect our mindset and the decisions we take in times of challenges.
4. Pessimism is a hindrance to determination, perseverance, and self-belief and the man who spends his time

with pessimistic people is unknowingly heading for failure.
5. Indeed, we will all go through one adversity or the other in our life's journey but when you keep company with people who are always pessimistic and complaining about their adversities, it will not be long before you will start being pessimistic and doubtful about your ability to succeed amid your difficulties.
6. Your association matters a lot. You cannot be optimistic if you spend too much time with pessimistic people. You can't be positive when you are always in the company of negative people. It is difficult to walk forward in the company of people who are walking backward.
7. One of the greatest secrets to overcoming adversity is to walk with people who encourage, inspire, and are going in the same direction as you.
8. Why should I be in the company of people who kill hope, destroy initiatives and discourage dreams when I could

spend the same time with people who encourage, inspire, and energizes me to walk in the direction of my dreams!

9. You will begin to doubt your natural talents, skills, and shrewdness if you allow mediocre people to dictate what you can or can't do.
10. In times of adversity, you need people that will push you in the direction of your dreams, people that can synergize your potential to overcome that adversity and those who believe in you.

Chapter Five

You Are Not an Island

Chapter Five
You Are Not an Island

There is no greater secret to success in business than having the right people working with you and for you. When you have the right team, you will much easier handle adversity, overcome it, and succeed despite it. In this chapter, we shall discuss how having the right team doesn't only increase business success but also help overcome adversity.

Build a Passionate Team

One common mistake people often make in business is thinking that they can become successful entrepreneurs by themselves. Having had enough experience in business, I advise against such a mindset and strongly refute that ideology. The reason is that no man can succeed all by himself. No man is an island. If we need people to succeed under normal circumstances, how much more do we need them in times of adversity! No matter how smart you think you are, you need a partner or a team if you want to build a successful business and overcome adversity.

None of us is as smart as all of us."
--Ken Blanchard

Imagine if I was struggling all by myself and going through my special needs parenting journey alone. What do you think would have happened? I would not have made it this far if I was walking this difficult road alone. None of us can succeed all by ourselves especially when we have one or two adversities that we are battling with. That is why we need a team to work with. No matter how smart, talented, or passionate you are, your success as an entrepreneur especially in times of adversity depends on how well you can build and inspire a team. Your success in business depends largely on your ability or inability to build and inspire a team to achieve the vision and goals of the company. I reiterate "If you want to succeed in business, you must build a team but not just any kind of team." You need a passionate team. You need a team that understands the vision and goals of your company and are ready to run with them, sacrifice and put in the hard work needed to achieve those goals and actualize those visions. Besides building a passionate team for business success, it is also always good for you to build relationships that will be able to motivate you in times of adversity. Whether you like it or not there will be times that you might lack motivation and the will power to go forward in the direction of your dreams because of the challenges you will encounter. However, having shared your vision with loved ones, they will be able to help you on those days, during those tough times. Remember that no man is an island.

Don't Try to Do Everything on Your Own

I discovered early on in my business journey as a parent, disability advocate, and entrepreneur, that I cannot succeed amid adversity on my own, and thanks to that discovery, I built a team. If you desire to be a successful entrepreneur, you need to find passionate and trustworthy partners to work with. For me, my husband is my number one partner. My husband and I have always worked together because I realized that to be successful one cannot be an island. One of the erroneous ideologies that have become famous in recent times is the idea of independence or being self-made. Those mindsets that make people think that they can survive in this world alone without the help of others are the reason many people fail in times of adversity. The belief that you can overcome your challenges, setbacks, hurdles, limitations, and difficult circumstances by yourself is not only delusional but also dangerous. It would do you more harm than good. The earlier you recognize that you need help from others and that we were created for each other the better for you. None of us have what it takes to overcome our challenges without help. None of us have what it takes to build a successful business without a team or a partner. We need other people on our journey to success.

You and I were created to live interdependently and not in isolation.

Life doesn't make any sense without interdependence. We need each other, and the sooner we learn that the better for us all.

-Erik Erikson

Most people fail in life and faint in times of adversity simply because they try to do everything or handle their challenges all by themselves. They often try to cover their shame or hide their pains from others and thanks to that, build walls around themselves to shield them from everyone else. Oftentimes because of pride, people are afraid of opening up and asking for help in their times of difficulties. What they fail to understand is that no man is an island; no human was created to exist alone and bear his burden alone. That is why the biblical injunction said" Bear you one another's burden and so fulfill the law of Christ" What does this mean? It means that we should carry each other's burdens, challenges, and difficulties. Why? It is because none of us can bear our burdens alone. None of us can succeed without the help of others. We were created to depend on each other. That is why you shouldn't try to do everything by yourself. If you do, you will wear yourself out before you know it. You will overwork yourself and still not be able to overcome your adversity and challenges if you try to do everything by yourself.

What do you think would happen to my business, family, and career if I tried to take care of my special needs children, my business, and political career all alone without the help of a partner or a team? I would fail woefully! So, the reason I succeeded and still succeeding in my business and career despite being a special needs parent is that I learned not to do everything by myself. I learned to partner and work with other positive-minded people. I usually advise people to, get smart, intelligent, and passionate partners who would run with the vision of the company or business organization. Your husband, wife, brothers, sisters, or friends could be your partners as long as they have the required know-how to succeed on the job.

Alone we can do so little, together we can do so much
-Helen Keller

For me, I worked with people that are even outside my family circle. When my business got to a point, in terms of expansion I had to start looking into hiring because I realized I could not handle everything by myself. Before this time, I had thought "I don't need a staff, I can do everything by myself," However, I got overwhelmed by the work demands and realized that if I was going to succeed, I needed to hire others to work with me.
 So in terms of building relationships, I advocate that business owners, entrepreneurs should not be afraid to reach out and ask for help from family members, peers, advisors, and mentors. No matter how talented or experienced you are, you can't do everything on your own. I have over the years built and fortified myself up to a level that I could

succeed in business. However, I still needed a team to help me because I realized that multinational companies are not run by a single person but by a team. Therefore, it is important as a business owner who wants to overcome adversity and succeed to try to collaborate. Don't try to do everything on your own. Even if you think that you are a master of all trades, there will be some aspects that other people or your partner will be good at and thus, it will help you to leverage your entrepreneurial success.

Before You Hire

Before closing this chapter, I would like to give you one successful business secret that has helped me achieve much of my business goals. When you have gotten to the point where it is necessary to expand your business, you must be careful with hiring. The nature or quality of people we hire could either negatively or positively affect our business. That is why you must be very careful who you hire to work for you. Only trustworthy,

skillful, and passionate people should be on your employee's list if you must build a business that will last. The fact that we said you need people to succeed does not mean you can just hire anybody to be in your team. You must be selective when you are hiring. Successful business owners employ the best workers in their team. To excel as an entrepreneur, you need highly skillful, knowledgeable, motivated, and optimistic people in your team. Hiring was a core part of my business that I had to carefully look into because the nature or quality of people you hire can affect your business in unimaginable ways. Whether in business or life as a whole, there are nine categories of people you need to keep you going in the direction of your dreams especially in times of adversity.
John Addison in one of his writings said that every successful person needs these nine vital roles in his or her life. He identified these as:

The Believer
When you feel fear and self-doubt creeping into your mind, The Believer is there to

remind you of your capabilities. Don't confuse this with someone who tells you only what you want to hear. That doesn't help anyone improve. The Believer can be a parent, spouse, best friend, or business partner, who knows where you started and where you are now. This person is realistic about your accomplishments and isn't afraid to speak up when you're wrong. The Believer knows your potential and will be a positive force when negativity clouds your brain.

The Teacher
Winston Churchill is my greatest inspiration and my greatest teacher. I think he's so inspiring because of his stance on failure — another great teacher. "Success is not final, failure is not fatal; it is the courage to continue that counts," he said. How powerful is that? You will fail a million times in your life. But what if you took each of those failures as an opportunity to learn and grow and act differently? Churchill lived that principle. Your Teacher can be someone from history, a respected elder, or someone in the cubicle next

to you. But the bottom line is this: When the Teacher is speaking, listen.

The Pusher
A pusher is someone who pushes you to be better by example.
Your parents or whoever spurs you to success is your pusher. A pusher will teach you patience, kindness, and communication. A Pusher is not someone who leads with an iron fist, who inspires with fear. It's someone who pushes you to succeed by showing you how.

The Lover
Don't get caught up on the title of this one. The Lover isn't always a romantic person, but someone who is your biggest supporter. The lover keeps your best interests at heart at all times because he or she loves you. Now don't get The Lover confused with someone who will blindly follow you on any path you choose. The Lover is the first person to remind you that it's time to slow down, re-evaluate, reprioritize, and strategize. He or she is also the person who listens patiently when you

need to talk through a tough decision in the middle of the night. You ought to cherish these people. They will be your rock.

The Thinker
There is always one person in a group who seems to have all of the answers. You need such a person in your team. He's not a know-it-all but an intelligent person. He's a listener, a watcher, a thinker. He takes a moment to gather the facts, organize, and analyze them. This person balances out the dreamer in us. When we want to rush full-speed ahead, they pause to make sure the data makes sense. Listen to this person. Include them in all of your big decisions and you would have more successes in your business.

The Achiever
Everyone comes across someone in their lives who inspires them to dream bigger than they once did. An achiever is someone who acts as a benchmark of success for you. He doesn't laze about but works hard to succeed. Such persons do not accept failure because they get

up from their fall and keep walking towards success. We've all experienced failure throughout our careers and this friend is no different. Instead of caving to the thought of I can't do this, he stands up and finds a new (and often better) path. The Achiever is the photo on your vision board, the motivation when obstacles arise, the mutual celebration when you succeed.

The Anchor
You need an anchor if you want to overcome adversity and achieve success in business. Your anchor will help you handle your chaotic schedule. When you are eager to say yes to any opportunity that seems like it could benefit your career, your anchor is the voice in your ear that says, "We can't say yes to everything." The Anchor is realistic, grounded, trusted, and reliable. They often know you better than you know yourself. They know your limits. They understand when a great opportunity isn't great right now. Treat this person with respect, and

they'll be your guiding force to achieving your dreams.

The Scale
Work-life balance is almost a cliché. We hear advice on all sides about where to be for how long, what to prioritize, and how to leave work at the door. But the truth is, balance is personal. What works in my life could never work for a 23-year-old single parent. We have different dreams, priorities, and realities that simply don't fit in the same box. The Scale is your priority. My kids are my priority. They are the inspiration behind my brand and I would let go of everything else to make sure they are happy, strong and healthy.

Fighter
Fighters are fierce but not aggressive. They are the cornerstone of a solid team. The Fighter might be your top employee. For me, it wasn't one person, but a type of person. Whenever I hired a new team member, the interview process wasn't just a conversation between the two of us. My team of other Fighters needed to meet the potential candidate because they can

sense the spark of intensity in another Fighter. Loyalty isn't about fear; it's about trust, communication, and transparency. I wanted this person to see my company from the inside out. We're not just making sure they're a good fit for us, but that we are a good fit for them. After all, a company is only as strong as its weakest link.[1]

In conclusion, I want you to know that if you want to overcome adversity and succeed as an entrepreneur and in your life generally, you must realize that no man is an island and that you need people to succeed.

Nuggets Five

1. There is no greater secret to success in business than having the right people working with you and for you. When you have the right team, you will much easier handle adversity, overcome it, and succeed despite it.

2. If we need people to succeed under normal circumstances, how much more do we need them in times of adversity! No matter how smart you think you are, you need a partner or a team if you want to build a successful business and overcome adversity.

3. None of us can succeed all by ourselves especially when we have one or two adversities that we are battling with. That is why we need a team to work with.

4. No matter how smart, talented, or passionate you are, your success as an

entrepreneur especially in times of adversity depends on how well you can build and inspire a team.
5. That mindset that makes people think that they can survive in this world alone without the help of others is the reason many people fail in times of adversity.
6. The belief that you can overcome your challenges, setbacks, hurdles, limitations, and difficult circumstances by yourself is not only delusional but also dangerous. It would do you more harm than good.
7. None of us have what it takes to overcome our challenges without help. None of us have what it takes to build a successful business without a team or a partner.
8. Most people fail in life and faint in times of adversity simply because they try to do everything or handle their challenges all by themselves.

9. None of us can succeed without the help of others. We were created to depend on each other. That is why you shouldn't try to do everything by yourself. If you do, you will wear yourself out before you know it.
10. Only trustworthy, skillful and passionate people should be on your employee's list if you must build a business that will last.

Chapter Six

First Things First

Chapter Six
First Things First

While we all need to work hard and strive to succeed in business and life in general, we must never do that at the expense of our well-being. In this chapter, we shall discuss how to put first things first as we journey towards achieving our business and career goals.

Health, Happiness, and Well-Being

While we all as business people want to succeed and grow our business, we mustn't overwork ourselves so much so that we endanger our health and wellbeing. What is the use of having a great business when it is at the detriment of your health and wellbeing? One strategy to overcoming adversity in your life and business is for you to prioritize your health, happiness, and well-being. While this ought to be common knowledge, it is however common to see people who prioritize their paycheck and work deadlines above their health and wellbeing. This has led to many health challenges and even death.

Japan has become famous for a phenomenon called "karoshi," the sudden deaths of ostensibly healthy people from periods of intense, unbroken work. The concept stretches back to the 1980s, but recent cases include a 31-year-old woman who died after working 159 hours of overtime in one month.

Of course, "karoshi" is not limited to Japan's borders; wherever people are overworking, it looms. In London in 2013, for example, an intern at Bank of America died after reportedly working for 72 hours straight. Just as with physical injuries, work can cause subtler damage to our sleep schedules, the repercussions adding up slowly, like sand in an hourglass. Studies show that lack of sleep or poor sleep quality can cause anxiety, a lack of control over emotions, physical pain, and impulsive behavior, which can lead to eating or drinking too much.

Prolonged stress causes cortisol release and if this happens for extended periods, it can wreak havoc on our organs.

It's the heart that seems especially vulnerable to the demands of the workplace. In 2010, a study in the European Heart Journal showed that British employees who worked 10 or more hours a day were more likely to have heart problems than their peers who worked 7 hours a day. Work provides the means to live, but it's increasingly clear that the modern workplace can kill too.[1]

Dear friend, as you work hard to overcome the adversities of life and make ends meet, you must never forget that whatever success you are looking for is only possible if you are alive. A dead man cannot talk about business or career success. There are no entrepreneurial medals of honor in the grave. Money, success, recognition, net worth, etc. are only things we can acquire while we live. After death, everything becomes meaningless. This is the reason you must prioritize your health above everything else. Do not overwork yourself.

Know your limits and do not overstretch yourself! You do not want to complicate your adversities with additional health challenges that result from excessive stress.

Besides prioritizing your health, you must also prioritize your happiness. If you are working at a job that you dislike or that steals your happiness, you will hardly be able to excel and overcome adversity.

"Happiness is the meaning and the purpose of life, the whole aim and end of human existence."
—Aristotle

Although I am engaged with a lot of things, I prioritize my health, happiness, and well-being. I try not to exceed my limit. This is one strategy that has helped me to excel in my business and career. Most of the strategies I am writing about in this book are not strategies that were developed overnight; these skills have been honed and fine-tuned over the years. Knowing how to prioritize my health and well-being is a particular aspect that I have had to work extra hard on because, like most mothers, even as a special needs mother, I tend to put the needs of my children above mine. Because of the nature of the complex disabilities that my children especially my daughter is faced with, I knew I had to make them my priority. So, while I still pursue business and career success, I have learned to slow down and pay attention to my health and that of my children. I realized early on that if I overwork myself and develop a serious medical condition as a result, I would not be the only one to bear the effect of that but my children as well. I would not be strong enough to take care of them or pursue the success that I so much desire. It is therefore very important to consider your health and wellbeing as you work hard to overcome your challenges and gain success in business. You must prioritize your health and well-being irrespective of the goals and dreams you seek to achieve. Remember that only those who are hale and hearty can pursue success and achieve their dreams.

You Need To Be Hale And Hearty

It doesn't matter what most motivational speakers say about the need to work round the clock to achieve unimaginable success, I still believe that our health, well-being, and happiness should come first before anything else. While I believe that hard work is necessary to achieve exceptional results, I, however, would not overwork myself to the point where my health and wellbeing are affected negatively. I do not also advise people to wear themselves out just because they want to achieve the business success that no one else has achieved before. Who will enjoy that success when you endanger your health and eventually die from stress and its complications? You have to be hale and hearty to be able to build a successful business and career.

There are many perks of being the head honcho, but the toll of pursuing success in entrepreneurship can also be enormous if you don't protect your biggest asset: your well-being. Below are 10 common health issues entrepreneurs face:

1. *Depression*: In a recent landmark study by Dr. Michael Freeman, a clinical professor at UCSF and entrepreneur, 49% of the more than 240 entrepreneurs surveyed reported having a mental health condition, with depression as the No. 1 reported condition among them.

2. *Anxiety*: Dr. Freeman's study also indicated that 27% of entrepreneurs surveyed indicated issues with anxiety. That's more than the whole U.S. population, (at a rate of 18.1%.)

3. *Addiction:* Recent research has found that habitual entrepreneurs display symptoms of behavioral addiction similar to other traditional behavioral addictions, such as gambling or internet usage. Symptoms can include obsessive thoughts and sometimes there are negative emotional outcomes such as guilt, high levels of strain, and abuse of foods, alcohol or even drugs.

4. Hypertension/Heart Disease: It's no secret that being responsible for the financial prosperity of others as well as the overall success of a business can be quite stressful. High stress has been shown to temporarily heighten blood pressure and can trigger habits such as unhealthy eating which can lead to heart disease.

5. Lack of Health Insurance: A recent Gallup-Healthways analysis conducted for The New York Times found entrepreneurs are less likely to have health insurance, with solopreneurs in particular often have to choose between covering everyday necessities vs. paying high monthly insurance premiums.

6. Joint and Circulation Challenges: Entrepreneurs have been found to work 63% longer than the average worker, and many spend a lot of that time at a desk, behind a computer or on their smartphones: a welcome environment for circulation and joint challenges.

7. Sleeping Disorders: With a large percentage of founders working at least 52 hours per week (with some even working a whopping 70 hours), there's not much time left for sleep. Experts recommend 6 to 8 hours of sleep a day, but entrepreneurs working long hours are getting more like 4 to 6 hours. Also, issues like insomnia and jet lag are common with busy CEOs.

8. Vision-Related Problems: The average adult spends 11 hours per day on gadgets, and entrepreneurs are more than attached to their smartphones, laptops, and computers. And there is such a thing as computer vision syndrome, also referred to as digital eye strain.

9. Migraines: Of course, being an entrepreneur doesn't directly cause migraines, however, many of the triggers for them have been found to be a weekly norm for ambitious startup stars.

10. Sexual Health: Stress, anxiety, and depression have all been linked to issues such as erectile dysfunction and hormone suppression in women. They can also have an opposite effect, leading to unsafe sexual behavior which can lead to risk for STDs[2]

I cannot stress it enough that first things must come first. Your health and wellbeing must come first as you strive to overcome adversity and pursue entrepreneurial success. I had thought otherwise and that success in business comes first before anything else. I didn't know that I had to prioritize my business and career success above my health.

I, however, learned the importance of prioritizing my health only after I had made the mistake of ignoring my well-being and paying a heavy price for it. I learned in a hard way and by experience. I reached the point where I had to have surgery for health reasons because I perhaps wasn't eating the right things nor paying attention to exercise. It happened because I was focused on caring for others and not looking after myself. You do not have to repeat my mistakes. You can simply learn from my story on how not to prioritize business success above your health. My story is just one of many of how people suffer different health challenges as they struggle to gain or achieve huge success in their businesses and career

I thus warn those who come to me for counseling not to make the mistake of putting the last things first and first things last. The result of turning the pattern upside down is not only maligning but deadly.

We all need to be hale and hearty first before we could overcome adversity or build successful businesses.

"It's up to you today to start making healthy choices. Not choices that are just healthy for your body, but healthy for your mind."
— *Steve Maraboli*

There is this caring mindset that often actually develops as a result of your parenting experience in the sense that you tend to even subconsciously, put your energy into your child so much so that you can easily forget yourself and yes, that was exactly what I did.

This is the reason why I need to put this out there so that others can learn from my mistakes. It is really important if we must be successful; to prioritize our well-being and I know that it is not easy. Practically a lot of parents, a lot of entrepreneurs and even special needs parents will tell you that they don't usually have the time to rest. So yes, I am acknowledging the fact that it is going to be very difficult especially if you are juggling a lot like me. But I want to say that you also certainly cannot pour from an empty cup. You need to replenish your energy by setting aside time to rest and refresh yourself. One of the reasons I was able to build a successful business amid my adversities is that I learned to prioritize my health, happiness, and well-being.

Striking a Balance is Key

The question therefore from the foregoing is how to strike a balance between our desire to excel and succeed in business and maintaining a healthy life. While the pressure to make more money and grow our businesses seems to overwhelm us, I often encourage people to learn to strike a balance between their work, career, business, and their well-being. While it is good to work diligently to achieve success, it is important to try to achieve some sort of balance. Create time to rest even if you are a small business owner who may tend to want to work around the clock with no holidays. You can try to cultivate that sort of habit where you could, for instance, take out a day in a week to isolate yourself from the hustle and bustle of life and rest. You could just shut your laptop and try to unwind. You could even go for a walk or just get some fresh air. There's also been lots of talk about sleep, quality of sleep and this is something that over the years has worked for me. No matter how busy I get, I make sure I find time to have quality sleep. If I am strategizing on a particular direction or new product to launch in my business or even in my life as a politician, if I need to chair a meeting and I am brainstorming on ideas, I find that going to bed early and having a good night sleep helps me to wake up refreshed and then the ideas just flow better in the morning. So actually overworking yourself late into the night and not giving your mind time to be refreshed is not actually beneficial because we tend to think we should as human beings just work hard. Well actually, you should work smart. If you are constantly drained, there is a likelihood that it would translate into failure in both your health or your life or your parenting. So yes, actually prioritizing our well-being and health is important.

Before closing this chapter, I would like to share with you 20 tips that will help you strike a balance between pursuing business or work success and maintaining health and wellbeing. Ella Legg, the founder of copywriting consultancy Ella Smith Communications, knows how difficult it can be to strike that balance and has put together these 20 tips for achieving and maintaining a healthy work/life balance.

Play to your strengths
Don't try and be all things to all people. Focus on your strengths and outsource the others. If you're not a whiz at accounts or graphic design, outsource them instead of wasting time.

Prioritize your time
You may have a to-do list with 50 tasks on it, so you need to prioritize those tasks into four categories.
They are:
Urgent and important
Important but not urgent
Urgent but not important
Neither urgent nor important.

Know your peaks and troughs
Are you a morning person?
If you are, assign tough, high-concentration tasks to the mornings. Don't leave the tough tasks until its night time and vice versa.

Plot some personal time

When personal issues arise, it can be tempting to bury yourself in your work. Don't do it If you don't make time for your personal life – your "me" time, including your family and your health – you won't have a business to go back to.

Have set work hours – and stick to them

Set work hours for yourself and do everything in your power to stick to them. Otherwise, before you know it, you'll be working until midnight every night.

Find time for your finances

Whether you work for yourself or not, it's important to feel confident about your finances. To do this, you need to get some accounting software in place and use it from day one.

Cash flow is one of the biggest challenges facing small businesses. You should start using accounting tools early on so you know what's going on, financially, from day dot.

Manage your time, long term

Create a timeline of your activities. Specific computer programs can help with this, or you can customize your own Excel spreadsheet or Word table. Put dates across the top and activities down the side. Break each task into components. Include family commitments – such as holidays, birthday parties, etc. – so you don't forget that you are unavailable for work on those days.

Make your workspace work for you

Working for yourself does tend to require long hours and not much downtime, so invest in equipment that will support you.
That includes getting a comfortable chair, an ergonomic keyboard, a support stand for your laptop, etc.
An ergonomic assessment of your workspace is worth every cent.

Tap into technology

Instead of driving to a meeting, use Skype or conferencing technologies like GoToMeeting. But remember to switch them off.

Make exercise a must-do, not a should-do
It's easy to cancel the gym, the evening run, or the yoga class because a client wants something done yesterday.
Instead, ensure the exercise is given as much priority as your clients and making money. A healthy body means a fresh mind, which means you will function better and complete tasks in less time.

Take time to make time
Invest in time-tracking tools. There are plenty of tools you can use to track everything from the frequency and duration of meetings to chasing and converting leads.
Time-tracking software allows you to quickly build an understanding of how long a particular task takes.
That way, you can effectively estimate how long your next work task will take.

Know and nurture your network
Prioritize growing your network and have a structured lead/conversion system in place so

you can track the time/cost involved to grow your network.
Set the benchmarks early on and learn the lessons early.

Do what you love
Make time for something you love – other than work – and give it the time it deserves. It will energize and refresh you, and enable you to nurture the creative thought that is essential to every business owner.

Be realistic
At the end of each working day, perform a little self-analysis. Ask yourself what worked today, what didn't, what went wrong, and how the issue can be fixed.
Remember there are thousands of businesses just like yours learning the same lessons every day. Don't forget to tap into the valuable resources around you – your peers – for help.

Step out
Working for yourself can get lonely, so schedule some phone calls or coffee time with

like-minded business owners to discuss ideas and offer each other support.

Get a business coach
Find the cash for a business coach. That way, you can find out sooner rather than later how to get rid of bad habits and implement good ones.

Meet clients halfway – literally
Don't always agree to meet a client at their office. Instead, meet halfway, perhaps at a café or restaurant. This will save you time and energy, not to mention the money spent on travel.

Manage your mind
When fear or self-doubt or anxiety creeps in, do some work on your mental health such as meditation or reading a business book. Alternatively, spend time with someone who will lift you up and support you.

Take a break

Remember to take time out throughout your day.

Some tasks are easier than others, so if you find yourself with an hour up your sleeve, be realistic about whether you can "afford" to rest or not. You might not have time every day to simply sit and "be", but do your best to give yourself a lunch break.

Also, make a point of getting up and stretching every 15 minutes. It will help you become clearer, more focused, and more productive.

Have that holiday

Make time for a holiday and book in breaks, at least quarterly. Even a long weekend every quarter is better than nothing.

But remember to advise your clients and customers as far in advance as possible.[3]

Nuggets Six

1. While we all as business people want to succeed and grow our business, we mustn't overwork ourselves so much so that we endanger our health and wellbeing.
2. As you work hard to overcome the adversities of life and make ends meet, you must never forget that whatever success you are looking for is only possible if you are alive. A dead man cannot talk about business or career success.
3. There are no entrepreneurial medals of honor in the grave. Money, success, recognition, net worth etc. are only things we can acquire while we live. After death, everything becomes meaningless. This is the reason you must prioritize your health above everything else.
4. You must prioritize your health and well-being irrespective of the goals and dreams you seek to achieve.

Remember that only those who are hale and hearty can pursue success and achieve their dreams.

5. While I believe that hard work is necessary to achieve exceptional results, I, however, would not overwork myself to the point where my health and wellbeing is affected negatively.
6. I cannot stress it enough that first things must come first. Your health and wellbeing must come first as you strive to overcome adversity and pursue entrepreneurial success.
7. We all need to be hale and hearty first before we could overcome adversity or build successful businesses.
8. One of the reasons I was able to build a successful business amid my adversities is that I learned to prioritize my health, happiness, and well-being.
9. While the pressure to make more money and grow our businesses seems to overwhelm us, I often encourage

people to learn to strike a balance between their work, career, business, and their well-being. While it is good to work diligently to achieve success, it is important to try to achieve some sort of balance.
10. Overworking yourself late into the night and not giving your mind time to be refreshed is not beneficial because we tend to think we should as human beings just work hard. Well actually, you should work smart.

Chapter Seven

You Are Not A Victim

Chapter Seven
You Are Not A Victim

In the previous chapter, we discussed the importance of maintaining a healthy lifestyle as we try to overcome adversity and achieve business and career success. In this chapter, we shall discuss how to get rid of the victim's mentality as we journey through adversity to greatness.

Get Rid of The Victim's Mentality

I have learned from my years of experience with adversity that it is self-destructive to walk around with a victim's mentality just because we suffered one or two adversities. The victim's mentality is a killer of potentials and initiatives. It limits one's human capacity and leaves one looking up to everyone else for help. Although we suffer adversity and unpleasant circumstances, yet we are not victims of circumstances and should not define ourselves as such. Although several events are going to happen in our lives that will cripple our joy, finances, and even our businesses, yet we must not define ourselves by the circumstances that happen to us.

"Today is a new day. Don't let your history interfere with your destiny! Let today be the day you stop being a victim of your circumstances and start taking action towards the life you want. You have the power and the time to shape your life. Break free from the poisonous victim mentality and embrace the truth of your greatness. You were not meant for a mundane or mediocre life!"
— Steve Maraboli

You are not a victim of circumstances; you are a person of purpose who has a destiny to fulfill and dreams to achieve. I know that sometimes, that feeling of guilt comes to remind us of our past and points us to how we are responsible for whatever it is we are currently experiencing. When that happens, remind yourself of the great future ahead of you. It doesn't matter if you actually are responsible for the difficult life that you perhaps are currently living. What matters is that you have resolved not to see yourself as a victim of circumstances but as a purpose-driven person with dreams to achieve and destiny to accomplish. I once felt like I was a victim and that my mistakes were responsible for my woes. That feeling that I was going through what I was going through because I had done something wrong was a display of my victim's mentality and it limited me for some time. I realized later on that the victim's mentality will only hold one down. It is of no advantage at all. It destroys business initiatives and productivity in almost all areas of life. If you want to be successful in life and overcome adversities, you must get rid of the victim's mentality.

Redefining your mindset

To live the life of your dreams, you must get rid of the victim's mentality and renew your mind. Your mindset goes a long way to affect the outcome of your life. I want you to know that one of the most important factors that influence our lives is our mindset and we must redefine how we view success, and how we look at our lives. I got to a place in my life where I said, Ok! I am a special needs parent but that is not all about my life. The fact that I have special needs children does not define me and what I can achieve with my life. That change of mindset from a victim to a purpose-driven and goal-oriented person that I am was what turned my life around. Instead of playing a victim all my life, I decided to take control of my life and maximize my potentials. Today, I am so much into many things: I am a politician, disability activist, property investor, entrepreneur and I run a special needs parenting group. I did not allow the victim's mentality to limit my potentials and stop me from achieving my dreams. I got rid of that mentality, redefined my worldview and paradigm, and started towards achieving my goals. Do not allow the victim's mentality to limit your potentials and stop you from achieving your dreams. Get rid of that mentality, redefine your worldview and paradigm, and start off towards achieving your goals.

You perhaps are thinking that challenges and setbacks in life are peculiar to you and that everyone else is doing just fine. I want you to know that it is not true. We all have adversities and unpleasant circumstances in our lives. I had said earlier in this book that everyone who is born into this world will struggle with one adversity or the other. The reason is that we do not have total control over life's happenings. No matter how careful and prudent we are, we cannot prevent certain events from happening to us. That is why we all go through adversity in life. Even if we are responsible for our ugly circumstances because of a mistake or two that we made in the past, it still doesn't warrant us living the rest of our lives with the victim's mindset and thereby limiting our future. Irrespective of who is responsible for your adversity, you must never allow that adversity to determine the direction of your life. Do not live a pitiable lifestyle because that is what mediocre people do. They want everyone to pity them and regard them as victims of life's ugly fate. You ought not to walk with such a mindset. You rather should do everything possible to overcome your adversity and achieve success despite it.

Even if you are born into adversity, do not see yourself as a victim. That was how you were born and you had no control over that. However, what the rest of your life will look like is completely up to you. You must learn to live beyond your affliction and adversities.

Beyond Affliction and Adversity

I cannot overemphasize the need to live beyond affliction and adversity. My life was full of adversities; from the birth of my daughter to the birth of my son with each of them having different health challenges that require serious medical attention and care. *Life keeps throwing me stones. And I keep finding the diamonds."*
– Ana Claudia Antunes

Despite all the adversities that plagued my life, I was able to excel in my business and political career. I believe that every person who is going through one adversity or the other can live beyond that adversity if they get rid of the victim's mindset and renew their minds.

Throughout my journey, adversity keeps coming to me. When I had my daughter I thought "yes, I had had enough". You know I was like "ah no, it wouldn't happen again". Even the bible says affliction will not rise a second time. Nevertheless, I do not view my daughter's disability as an affliction right now because my mind is renewed. But I know very well that there are a lot of religious folks who will look at her life and make conclusions about why she was born that way. It is true that she has been through a lot and even had a stroke recently. But in my mindset, I don't see it as an affliction anymore. Rather, I see her as a special needs child with a great destiny. Then my son was born 2 years after as a premature baby. Although he doesn't have a chromosomal disability like his sister, being born premature exposed him to a lot more medical conditions. He had a lot of complexities: his stomach wasn't digesting, he was very tiny, he wasn't breathing well, and he had bleeding in his brain and all sorts of things. When all these were happening, I was like, but why me? As an African woman, I said to myself as most Africans' often believe when the odds of life are against them "It must be that my ancestors have done something wrong" I said so because I didn't think that I have done anything in my life to warrant such adversities. So, yes, a lot of things have happened that have shaken me to my core. However, I have lived beyond all adversities, setbacks and ugly circumstances to fulfill my dreams, achieve success both in business and in politics. Today, even women who haven't had as much adversity as I have had in my life, look up to me for counsel. My life has become a source of inspiration and hope to many people as they see how a special need parent like me could achieve so much success in my life and business. How did I get to this stage of my life? It is by giving up the victim's mentality and deciding to live beyond my adversities. I took my adversities as an advantage to excel in different areas of my life. I often say to myself "If I could handle my adversities, then I can handle anything"

"Show me someone who has done something worthwhile, and I'll show you someone who has overcome adversity."
– Lou Holtz

From the foregoing, it is obvious that you too can live beyond adversity by simply getting rid of the victim's mentality and taking responsibility for the rest of your life. You can decide today, to pursue your dreams and ambitions despite whatever setbacks life has thrown at you. Use the skills you learned from handling your unpleasant circumstances as tools to succeed in life and business. You are not a victim; you are a success waiting to happen. Pursue your dreams! Defy adversity! Fulfill your destiny!

Nuggets Seven

1. I have learned from my years of experience with adversity that it is self-destructive to walk around with a victim's mentality just because we suffered one or two adversities. The victim's mentality is a killer of potentials and initiatives. It limits one's human capacity and leaves one looking up to everyone else for help.
2. Although we suffer adversity and unpleasant circumstances, yet we are not victims of circumstances and should not define ourselves as such. Although several events are going to happen in our lives that will cripple our joy, finances, and even our businesses, yet we must not define ourselves by the circumstances that happen to us.
3. You are not a victim of circumstances; you are a person of purpose who has a destiny to fulfill and dreams to achieve.

4. I know that sometimes, that feeling of guilt comes to remind us of our past and points us to how we are responsible for whatever it is we are currently experiencing. When that happens, remind yourself of the great future ahead of you.
5. It doesn't matter if you are responsible for the difficult life that you perhaps are currently living. What matters is that you have resolved not to see yourself as a victim of circumstances but as a purpose-driven person with dreams to achieve and destiny to accomplish.
6. I realized later on in life that the victim's mentality will only hold one down. It is of no advantage at all. It destroys business initiatives and productivity in almost all areas of life. If you want to be successful in life and overcome adversities, you must get rid of the victim's mentality.
7. Do not allow the victim's mentality to limit your potentials and stop you from

achieving your dreams. Get rid of that mentality, redefine your worldview and paradigm, and start off towards achieving your goals.

8. Irrespective of who is responsible for your adversity, you must never allow that adversity to determine the direction of your life.
9. Even if you are born into adversity, do not see yourself as a victim. That was how you were born and you had no control over that. However, what the rest of your life will look like is completely up to you. You must learn to live beyond your affliction and adversities.
10. I believe that every person who is going through one adversity or the other can live beyond that adversity if they get rid of the victim's mindset and renew their minds.

Chapter Eight

Immune to Adversity

Chapter Eight
Immune to Adversity

Before the time adversity became a part of my life, I had this mindset that I was sort of immune to major life challenges. How did I arrive at such conclusions? I kind of sense that this must have been a sort of feeling that I got from religion; constantly feeling that as long as I did everything right, as long as I was a good person, as long as I was a Christian, as long as I was serving God, I was completely immune to life's problems, adversities or challenges.

So, on the day my daughter was born and the doctors came to me and started saying all sorts of things about her life, about how her life was going to be difficult, and about her disabilities, I was shocked. To say I was shocked was an understatement. I thought, "why me? Why do I deserve this? Why was I chosen to be a mum to a child with a disability?"

Why did I feel that I was immune to adversities in the first place? There are a couple of reasons:

I felt that as long as I did everything right, as long as I tried to be a good person, be kind to others, be socially moral, I just assumed overtime that good things will always happen to me. Somehow, I got a wakeup call from such disillusionment. The wakeup call, even before my daughter was born, was when I lost my mum. I was eight months pregnant before I lost my mum and I had always set up this picture in my head of how my mother was going to fly over to the United Kingdom to stay by my side when I am giving birth and then she will help me babysit my daughter after she is born and then I can go straight away into working with a fantastic company. However, I didn't know that adversity was about to strike. Her death was completely unexpected and I was in for a rude shock. About 13 years ago when my mum passed, she was barely 48, that is barely 50 and I just thought, "No, she has unfinished business here, she was so young".

I know some of the things that she had talked to me about, her dreams, her aspirations, things she wanted to do unknowingly to her that she would exit the world soon. It was then I realized that actually, nobody can say that they know exactly when they would go. As a result of that, the value of my life, the value of my time, what I do with my time, the impact I make on this earth started to open up to me before my eyes. No matter what stumbling blocks we face, one day, we will all check out of this life. My mum's death was a wakeup call to me. Then a month after, I put to bed, before I even put to bed, I named my daughter Joy because I was expecting that everything will suddenly become rosy: I will become a mum and then I will forget everything. Not like forgetting my mum, but a whole new chapter was going to open for me. Little did I know that I was moving from frying pan to fire! My mum had just died and suddenly I was thrust into special needs parenting – an invitation that I didn't ask for. So I was in for a rude shock.

My mother's death and my daughter's birth were two life events that sort of woke me up in a way from that illusion of being immune to adversity.

Developing Yourself

There are many misconceptions out there about adversity and why it happens to people. It is a common ideology in Africa for example that unpleasant circumstances happen to people only because they have done something wrong in the past. I would love to refute that ideology that links adversity to the wrongs that people have done in their past. Adversities are not repercussions for some mistakes or offenses. If that were the case, then adversity would happen only to a few persons. However, we have said earlier that everyone born into this world goes through one form of adversity or the other.

Nobody is immune to adversity. We are all susceptible to challenges and adversity. My life story is proof of how anybody irrespective of religion, economic status, race, or political affiliation is prone to adversity.

While it is true that we all go through adversity and that no one is immune to it, our reaction or response is however different. Some people see adversity as the end of their lives and others as a reason to live a life of blame and mediocrity. Successful people, however, see adversity as an opportunity to develop themselves and learn new skills.

For every challenge you face in life, you ought to develop yourself to be able to withstand it. Evolutionary theory in biology explained how a period of adverse weather conditions caused giraffes to develop long necks. The French zoologist Jean-Baptiste Lamarck is usually credited as the first person to suggest that long necks have evolved in giraffes because they allow them to get to the parts other herbivores cannot reach. As the giraffe lives "in places where the soil is nearly always arid and barren, it is obliged to browse on the leaves of trees and to make constant efforts to reach them," he wrote in his 1809 book Philosophie Zoologique. "From this habit long maintained in its entire race, it has resulted that the animal's forelegs have become longer than its hind legs and that its neck is lengthened."[1]

From the above, we see that even animals develop new traits to withstand adverse conditions and survive nevertheless. If animals can do that, how much more humans! Instead of lamenting about adversity and shrinking away from it, you should rather use it as an opportunity to develop yourself. Develop yourself, it will speak volumes. The skills that you will learn from handling adversity would be some of the skills you would need very badly in the future as you pursue a business or other fields of life.
For me, I learned a lot of skills. Remember that I talked about being organized. It is a skill that still helps me today. If you want to be a successful entrepreneur, you must be organized. You must learn how to constantly write down new goals and plans. That was a skill I learned in my time of adversity. You can choose whatever skill you want to learn from adversity. The bottom line is that adversity is

an opportunity for you to develop new skills and become a better, wiser, and stronger person.

An Opportunity to Learn Something

We should all see adversity as an opportunity to learn something new and develop ourselves instead of as a punishment or repercussion for something bad that we've done.

"We don't develop courage by being happy every day. We develop it by surviving difficult times and challenging adversity."
– Barbara De Angelis

A key way to look at adversity is seeing every negative life event as an opportunity to learn something. When you go through adversity whether big or small, see it as an opportunity to learn something. There came a time when every single time I had a call from the hospital for my daughter it was always bad news: there is something wrong with her liver, something wrong with her kidney, this is wrong with this, all sorts of adversity. I learned patience, perseverance, courage, determination all thanks to adversity.

So, instead of thinking that adversity has come to destroy you, see every life's event as a learning opportunity, as a chance to learn and develop yourself. If you do, your whole world would just explode in terms of the knowledge and experience you would gain. When your mindset begins to change and you have developed yourself enough, then you are ready to face the world, you are ready to become a successful business or career personality. I know it sounds a bit cliché to say that learning leads to success. But, in my life, I can say to you that when you invest in yourself, you become a better person. If you know your areas of weakness and day by day make an effort to become better, you simply need to move a step today, move another step another day, constantly trying to invest in yourself until you overcome your weakness and turn them into strengths.

As I conclude this chapter, I want you to know that no one is immune to adversity no matter their position in society. Adversity comes to us all to help us develop and grow into stronger and better individuals.

Nuggets Eight

1. The value of your life, the value of your time, what you do with your time, the impact you make on this earth ought to be your major concern.
2. No matter what stumbling blocks we face, one day, we will all check out of this life.
3. Adversities are not repercussions for some mistakes or offenses. If that were the case, then adversity would happen only to a few persons. However, what is a fact is that everyone born into this world goes through one form of adversity or the other.
4. Nobody is immune to adversity. We are all susceptible to challenges and adversity.
5. While it is true that we all go through adversity and that no one is immune to it, our reaction or response is however different. Some people see adversity as the end of their lives and others as a

reason to live a life of blame and mediocrity. Successful people, however, see adversity as an opportunity to develop themselves and learn new skills.

6. Instead of lamenting about adversity and shrinking away from it, you should rather use it as an opportunity to develop yourself.

7. Develop yourself, it will speak volumes. The skills that you will learn from handling adversity would be some of the skills you would need very badly in the future as you pursue a business or other fields of life.

8. Adversity is an opportunity for you to develop new skills and become a better, wiser, and stronger person.

9. See adversity as an opportunity to learn something new and develop yourself instead of as a punishment or repercussion for something bad that you've done.

10. Instead of thinking that adversity has come to destroy you, see every life's event as a learning opportunity, as a chance to learn and develop yourself. If you do, your whole world would just explode in terms of the knowledge and experience that you would gain.
11. If you know your areas of weakness and day by day make an effort to become better, you simply need to move a step today, move another step another day, constantly trying to invest in yourself until you overcome your weaknesses and turn them into strengths.

Chapter Nine

Pushing Through Adversity

Chapter Nine
Pushing Through Adversity

In this chapter, we shall discuss how and why you should push through adversity instead of giving up your dreams and goals for it.

Don't Stop, Time is Still Moving

While it is true that adversity makes us stronger and better individuals, some people still see adversity as a stop signal and hence halt their entire life just because of one or a few adversities. Do not let adversity put a stop to your life goals and ambitions. Successful people push through adversity. They do not allow adversity to stop their life's journey.

I have pushed through adversity and I want to tell you that it is possible to push through adversity no matter the kind of or scope of adversity that you face.

The only way to not let adversity stop your life's journey is to focus on your goals, dreams, and life's purpose while handling or trying to contain whatever adversity you are battling with.

"Instead of focusing on that circumstance that you cannot change – focus strongly and powerfully on the circumstances that you can."
– Joy Page

If you look carefully, you will find that life goes on, no matter the challenges that you are facing. So, why should you give up on your dreams? No matter the adversity that you are facing, life is not going to stop because of it, life still goes on. This should be your motivation to keep moving, to keep going, and keep fulfilling your ambitions, dreams, and purpose. Until life stops, you shouldn't stop dreaming and aiming at your goals. You were born for a purpose and you do not want to stop pursuing the fulfillment of that purpose because of one or two adversities. You have a dream and an ambition; you do not want to surrender it all to adversity that is surmountable. You will not find a successful person on this side of eternity that has not at some point in his or her life had to deal with adversity. The temptation to surrender all our dreams for the sake of setbacks, hindrances, and hurdles is a universal feeling. Those who yield to it end up miserably with little or no achievements. But those who realize that adversity is part of life and an avenue to learn skills and traits for future success keep on going in the direction of their dreams until they eventually win, succeed and accomplish their goals.

"There are many people in the world who have succeeded in climbing the ladder of achievement. Some of these people have persevered throughout their career having met what appeared insurmountable obstacles yet overcame these challenges to keep moving forward."
– Byron Pulsifer

As long as life continues, do not quit chasing your dreams; do not quit aiming at success. I learned in my times of adversity that life didn't stop because I have one or a few difficulties.

When I looked at time, I realized that it is infinite, in the sense that … I am almost 40 today, at a time I was almost 30, at a time I was almost 20, at a time I was almost 10. You find that life goes on. No matter the challenges you are facing, no matter the adversity you are facing, life is not going to stop. You will find that life is going on and in a way, it should be a motivation to keep moving, to keep going. Oh, I am going through something that feels as if my whole life is over and I should stop. But actually, time is still moving on, Monday is still going to come, Tuesday is still going to come, Wednesday is still going to come, Thursday is still going to come. So if life is not going to stop then why should I stop trying? So you have to constantly continue to strive as long as you have breath.

You will win if you don't quit

Before bringing this chapter to a close, I want to let you know that, to push through adversity, and emerge victoriously, you must never quit because quitters never win and those who win never quit. Most people often give up on their dreams in times of adversity but the few who do not eventually win. Keep faith alive and be patient, one day, you will win and that adversity will be no more. That was exactly what happened to Stephen King. Stephen king, the famous American writer was a man who saw adversity and was tempted to quit. However, he was able to believe in his dreams and waited patiently until his adversities were over.

King's most renowned and first book, Carrie, was rejected thirty times. King decided to toss the book, which his wife then went through the trash to rescue and convinced him to re-submit it.[1]

King modeled Carrie White after two of the loneliest girls he remembered from high school but Carrie turned out to be a very difficult book to write. When King started, he typed three single-spaced pages, crumpled them up in anger, and dumped them in the trash can. He was disappointed in himself. The whole story disgusted him. Worse yet, the process moved too slowly, which meant the finished product would be too long for any magazine.

"I couldn't see wasting two weeks, maybe even a month, creating a novella I didn't like and wouldn't be able to sell," King wrote in his memoir On Writing. "So I threw it away … After all, who wanted to read a book about a poor girl with menstrual problems?"

The next day, Tabby went to empty the trash in the laundry room and found three crinkled balls of paper. She reached in, brushed off a coat of cigarette ashes, and unwrinkled the pages. When King came home from work, she still had them.

"You've got something here," she said. "I really think you do." Over the next few weeks, Tabby guided her husband through the world of women, giving tips on how to mold the characters and the famous shower scene. She helped him rebuild his faith again and he continued to patiently develop the material. Nine months later, King had polished off the final draft.

Thirty publishers rejected it. I mean thirty publishers rejected it!

One day while King was at his workplace, his wife called his office. His secretary got the call and beckoned on King to come to receive the call from his wife.

When King picked up the phone, both he and Tabby were out of breath. She told him that the editor at Doubleday Publishing, Bill Thompson, had sent a telegram:

"Congratulations. Carrie officially a Doubleday book. Is $2500 advance okay? The future lies ahead. Love, bill."

King had broken through. The $2500 advance wasn't huge—not enough to quit teaching and pursue writing full time—but it was the most money he had ever made from writing.

King hoped that fat royalty checks would keep replenishing his bank account, but Carrie only sold 13,000 copies as a hardback, tepid sale that convinced him to grudgingly sign a new teaching contract for the 1974 school year.

He started a new novel called The House on Value Street, and, by Mother's Day, he figured Carrie had run its course. It was the last thing on his mind.

One phone call changed all that. It was Bill Thompson again. "Are you sitting down?" he asked.

King was home alone, standing in the doorway between his kitchen and living room. "Do I need to?" he said.

"You might," Thompson said. "The paperback rights to Carrie went to Signet Books for $400,000 ... 200K of it is yours. Congratulations, Stephen."

King's legs wobbled and gave out. He sat on the floor, shaking with excitement from winning the literal lottery. To cut the long story short, Carrie sold over 1 million copies in its first year as a paperback. King went on to become the 19th best-selling author of all time. When King was invited to speak at the national books award in 2003, he didn't talk about writing or success or money. He talked about the woman who rescued Carrie from the trash and insisted he keeps going—Tabby. "There is a time in the lives of most writers when they are vulnerable when the vivid dreams and ambitions of childhood seem to pale in the harsh sunlight of what we call the real world," King said at the ceremony. "In short, there's a time when things can go either way. That vulnerable time for me came from 1971 to 1973. If my wife had suggested to me even with love and kindness and gentleness ... that the time had come to put my dreams away and support my family, I would have done that with no complaint."

But the thought never crossed her mind. And if you open any edition of Carrie, you'll read the same dedication: "This is for Tabby, who got me into it—and then bailed me out of it."[2]

Why did I share this story with you? It is because I wanted you to see that adversity is not the end of life and that if you do not quit you will eventually win. If you do not abandon your dreams to adversity, they will eventually materialize. Had I quit and given up to adversity, I would not be this successful today. If you do not want to be a mediocre and a failure, you must learn to never quit in the days of adversity. Just like Stephen King, your days of adversity would be over and you will win if you didn't quit.

Nuggets Nine

1. Do not let adversity put a stop to your life goals and ambitions. Successful people push through adversity. They do not allow adversity to stop their life's journey.

2. The only way to not let adversity stop your life's journey is to focus on your goals, dreams, and life's purpose while handling or trying to contain whatever adversity you are battling with.

3. If you look carefully, you will find that life goes on, no matter the challenges that you are facing. So, why should you give up on your dreams?

4. No matter the adversity that you are facing, life is not going to stop because of it, life still goes on. This should be your motivation to keep moving, to keep going, and keep fulfilling your ambitions, dreams, and purpose.

5. Until life stops, you shouldn't stop dreaming and aiming at your goals. You were born for a purpose and you

do not want to stop pursuing the fulfillment of that purpose because of one or two adversities.
6. You have a dream and an ambition; you do not want to surrender it all to adversity that is surmountable.
7. You will not find a successful person on this side of eternity that has not at some point in his or her life had to deal with adversity.
8. The temptation to surrender all our dreams for the sake of setbacks, hindrances, and hurdles is a universal feeling. Those who yield to it end up miserably with little or no achievements. But those who realize that adversity is part of life and an avenue to learn skills and traits for future success keep on going in the direction of their dreams until they eventually win, succeed and accomplish their goals.

9. As long as life continues, do not quit chasing your dreams; do not quit aiming at success.
10. Keep faith alive and be patient, one day, you will win and that adversity will be no more.
11. Adversity is not the end of life. If you do not quit you will eventually win. If you do not abandon your dreams to adversity, they will eventually materialize.

Chapter Ten

Overnight Success Is a Myth

Chapter Ten
Overnight Success Is a Myth

In this chapter, we shall discuss why there is no such thing as an overnight success and the need to work hard to achieve success.

Hard Work: The Mother of Success

In the final chapter of this book, I want to address the notion that success in life and business could happen overnight. Because we live in a digital generation, most people are disillusioned and think that success in life and business is spontaneous. Successful businesses take time to build. No one becomes rich and sustains that wealth without first going through the process of learning how to set up a business, manage that business, and make a profit. In addition to that, one must learn the skills of financial management, the art of doing business and how to work in a team or partnership, etc. All these require time. The idea that one can become successful overnight is therefore only a myth and is not practicable.

"I'm convinced that about half of what separates the successful entrepreneurs from the unsuccessful ones is pure perseverance."
 --Steve Jobs

All successes are products of hard work. If we must overcome adversity and become successful in life and business, we must resolve to work hard and do so smartly.

A dream doesn't become reality through magic; it takes sweat, determination and hard work.
-Colin Powell

One major barrier that prevents people from accepting adversity as part of life is our modern-day view of social media where you find that people are attracted to people who have overnight successes and actually, you will find that a lot of people who even others might view as overnight successes haven't told you what is beneath the iceberg. There has been hard work, sleepless nights working, and all sorts of things going on behind the scene, a lot of times over a while before they came out on top. But people rarely share that and I don't want to be like that. A lot of people admire me for what they view to be a success, but I constantly sometimes feel sorry for some people who don't understand that no, it wasn't overnight!

You have to be careful on social media so that you are not just constantly thinking, "everybody is doing this; everybody is doing great things…" You need to realize that nobody is sharing with you their behind –the-scene and that is the reason why so many people struggle to accept adversities.

There is a lot of research that shows that social media is also fueling depression and mental health and suicidal thoughts because some people seem as if they are behind in life, seeing others moving ahead. But actually, you should delve deep and say "how did they get there? Was it overnight? Was it in one day, in 24 hours"? No, it is usually a journey; don't let anyone deceive you into thinking that success comes overnight without a process of hard work and perseverance.

Adversities or problems are part of life. We must overcome them before we attain any form of success. No success happens overnight. It is only if you win a lottery that you can basically just talk about overnight success and even so, half of the time, and this is a rare occurrence; people who win lotteries usually just squander it. The reason is that obviously, the mindset to be able to manage that level of so-called material wealth which people do view erroneously as success is not there. It is only when we have gone through the process of learning and hard work that we can manage success in the right way. If you want to succeed, you must first learn hard work, perseverance, and determination. These are what adversity comes to teach us.

It's Too Early to Retire

So what happens when you have overcome adversity and achieved success? Do you retire? No! You do not need to retire. One success should lead to greater success. It is abnormal to relax or retire only after one success. People who become complacent after attaining a little height in life or business often lose everything they have when unexpected circumstances happen. However, if we repeat the processes that made us successful, we could replicate success and build a strong enough foundation that cannot be shaken when calamity strikes.

Although I have accrued so much success in my business and career, I still don't feel like I have reached that point where I can say yes, I am just going to retire on my goals. No! I am constantly moving in the direction of new dreams, new goals, and greater ambitions. To retire is to quit and conclude that there is nothing else that you could do with your life. Successful people hardly retire; they keep being a blessing and a source of hope to others. They dream again and again and do everything required to achieve those dreams. As I conclude this book, I want to remind you that adversity is part of life and that you ought not to run away from it but befriend it. No matter the difficulties that will come your way in your lifetime, remember that you can overcome them by simply believing in yourself, in your dreams, and by working hard to achieve them.

I do hope that as you practice the principles that are in this book, you will soon be on your way to achieving your dreams, building your business success, and fulfilling your life goals. See you at the top!

Conclusion

I recently got asked about how I manage to do so many things that I do. This isn't a surprising question, because I get it from time to time. Approximately 10 years ago when I received the inspiration to start my business, in my mind, I was hoping to be able to empower myself to lead a life of financial independence.

At the time, if anyone told me that my business was going to thrive beyond one year, I would have looked back at the person with surprise. All I had then was a sewing machine, overlocker, and my conservatory (aka office) but we haven't just thrived beyond year one, we are approaching approximately year ten in business.

The aspect of business that no one ever really prepares you for is the sudden onset of challenges, this can range from business, financial to personal problems. At the start of my business, I had to navigate the change of

running a business as an immigrant, living in a foreign unfamiliar environment.
There was a lot of learning to be done.
I started my business around the time that my almost eleven-year-old, Joseph, was born, so my business had to survive that phase of my life, in the neonatal intensive care unit. Joseph was that baby who spent most of his first year within the confines of the hospital. So in a way, adversity has always been a part and parcel of the Joy and Joe brand. We wanted families to understand that we are hoping to divert our pain into something positive, by encouraging as many families as possible to bond and create beautiful memories with their children.

Apart from complex health challenges that Joy and Joseph face, I had to navigate customer relation challenges. However, challenges such as royal mail misplacing your customer parcels or weaving loom breaking down weren't the major challenges that I have had to encounter.

Two years ago, I excitedly hinted our Joy and Joe customers with a cryptic announcement where I mentioned that our brand name might be changing. This was because we are an eponymous brand named after my two children, Joy and Joseph. I wanted to share the good news that we are expecting our third baby. I was about five months pregnant at the time and then suddenly, a rude shock, at five months, I miscarried my baby.

This experience has been the most brutal challenge that life has ever thrown my way, I'm generally not afraid of challenges. I was made to labor as normal and deliver my baby sleeping. I thought that the world was over. The business was the least on my mind at the time. Shortly after, Joy suffered a stroke. I didn't imagine that I would ever recover from the nightmare. I wanted to close my business at the time to focus on recovery. Now I realize that what I needed then, was rest and not quitting.

At the end of the day, I am still responsible for Joy and Joseph and a reminder that I have a host of families who have derived (and are still deriving) some happiness from bonding with their children, using our Joy and Joe baby slings.

I took a break from weaving and this also gave us a chance to manage our current unsold inventory from previous releases. Around the summer of last year, as we were driving past our village high street, we saw an advert for a building for sale. The old shop was owned by an elderly man, an upholsterer who was looking to retire.

We indicated our interest and bought the entire building. The top flat and downstairs are all part of our new HQ, but we are temporarily renting the upstairs flat out to our tenant and our Joy and Joe babywearing shop is downstairs.

Looking back now, I still feel quite hurt whenever I remember that my two-year son could easily be running around right now but, I'm glad that I paused my business to rest and not quit. As simple as using a babywearing demo doll is enough to bring back the flood of tears. On some days, I still need to occasionally step back and do other things like my political work or community activism that takes my mind away from my pain. Helping other people has been therapeutic for me as well.

I don't know what challenges you might be facing as an entrepreneur in your industry, but I want you to understand that there's likelihood that you simply need some rest or break. Like me, please do not quit.

Nuggets Ten

1. Successful businesses take time to build. No one becomes rich and sustains that wealth without first going through the process of learning how to set up a business, manage that business, and make a profit.

2. The idea that one can become successful overnight is only a myth and is not practicable.

3. All successes are products of hard work. If we must overcome adversity and become successful in life and business, we must resolve to work hard and do so smartly.

4. Don't let anyone deceive you into thinking that success comes overnight without a process of hard work and perseverance. No, it is usually a journey.

5. Adversities or problems are part of life. We must overcome them before we attain any form of success. No success happens overnight.

6. . It is only when we have gone through the process of learning and hard work that we can manage success in the right way.

7. If you want to succeed, you must first learn hard work, perseverance, and determination. These are what adversity comes to teach us.

8. People who become complacent after attaining a little height in life or business often lose everything they have when unexpected circumstances happen.

9. If we repeat the processes that made us successful, we could replicate success and build a strong enough foundation that cannot be shaken when calamity strikes.

10. To retire is to quit and conclude that there is nothing else that you could do with your life. Successful people hardly retire; they keep being a blessing and a source of hope to others. They dream

again and again and do everything required to achieve those dreams.

Reference

Chapter One

1. *https://www.hki.org/helen-kellers-life-and-legacy/*
2. *https://www.essentiallifeskills.net/overcoming-adversity.html*

Chapter Two

1. *https://www.businessnewsdaily.com/7929-entrepreneurs-personal-obstacles.html*
2. *https://www.themuse.com/advice/9-famous-people-who-will-inspire-you-to-never-give-up*
3. *https://www.entrepreneur.com/article/275969*

Chapter Four

1. *https://www.businessinsider.com/jim-rohn-youre-the-average-of-the-five-people-you-spend-the-most-time-with-2012-7*
2. *https://padmashankar.blogspot.com/2014/06/chickens-and-eagle.html*

Chapter Five

1. https://www.success.com/the-9-people-you-need-to-be-successful/

Chapter Six

1. https://www.popsci.com/work-death/
2. https://www.blackenterprise.com/10-common-health-issues-entrepreneurs-face/
3. https://www.roche.com/careers/our-locations/asia/india/service/folder/20_tips_for_maintain.htm

Chapter Eight

1. http://www.bbc.com/earth/story/20160629-giraffes-did-not-evolve-long-necks-to-reach-tall-trees#:~:text=The%20French%20zoologist%20Jean%2DBaptiste,parts%20other%20herbivores%20cannot%20reach.&text=%22natural%20selection%22.-,Long%2Dnecked%20giraffes%20were%20more%20likely%20to%20survive%20hard,than%20their%20short%2Dnecked%20rivals

Chapter Nine

1. *35 Famous People Who Were Painfully Rejected Before Making It Big,* https://thoughtcatalog.com/rachel-hodin/2013/10/35-famous-people-who-were-painfully-rejected-before-making-it-big/
2. *How Stephen King's Wife Saved Carrie and Launched His Career,* http://mentalfloss.com/article/53235/how-stephen-kings-wife-saved-carrie-and-launched-his-career

BLURB

We live in a world of adversities, a world of storms, troubles, difficulties, and challenges. From the day we are born until the day we die, we would encounter adversity and face difficult circumstances. There are no exceptions; the same wind blows on us all. While a large percentage of people give up on their dreams and allow adversity to defeat them, a few others defy adversity and walk their way to success and greatness. In this book, you will learn:

1. That Adversity is part of life and we must brace up for it.
2. How to cultivate a positive attitude amid adversity.
3. The importance of focusing on your purpose, vision, and dreams instead of focusing on adversity, setbacks, and challenges.
4. Why keeping the right association is the key to success in life and business.
5. How to build a passionate team for optimal business success.

6. How to get rid of the victim's mentality in times of adversity.
7. How not to quit when life's challenges buffet you.
8. Why hard work is a prerequisite for success in life and business.
9. The principles for overcoming adversity and setbacks in life and business.

The difference between the successful and the mediocre people in any society or nation is dependent largely on their ability to embrace adversity, defy adversity, and overcome adversity. Those who shrink from adversity, learn nothing new, neither do they discover their hidden strength. However, the courageous look adversity in the face, conquers it, and succeeds despite it. I believe that as you apply the principles in this book, you would not only overcome adversity but also accomplish your dreams and ambitions in great measures. See you at the top!

Printed in Great Britain
by Amazon